D1301085

World Change and
World Security

World Change and World Security

Edited by
Norman C. Dahl and
Jerome B. Wiesner

Contributors

Roy Jenkins
Willy Brandt
McGeorge Bundy
David A. Hamburg
Sigvard Eklund
Roberto de Oliveira Campos
Georgi A. Arbatov
Canon Burgess Carr
Robert S. McNamara
Frank Church

The MIT Press
Cambridge, Massachusetts,
and London, England

This book was set in IBM Univers by Eastern Composition, Inc. It was printed on
R & E Book and bound in Holliston Roxite by Alpine Press in the United States
of America.

Library of Congress Cataloging in Publication Data
Main entry under title:

World change and world security

   (MIT Bicentennial studies series; 5) Includes index.
   1. Economic history—1945-   —Addresses, essays, lectures. 2. International
economic relations—Addresses, essays, lectures. 3. Underdeveloped areas—Addresses
essays, lectures. 4. Security, International—Addresses, essays, lectures. 5. World
politics—1965-   —Addresses, essays, lectures. I. Dahl, Norman C. II. Wiesner,
Jerome Bert, 1915-
HC59.W633   330.9'04   78-19037
ISBN 0-262-04058-1

Contents

1

2

3

4

**MIT Bicentennial
Studies Series**

As part of its contribution to the celebration of the U.S. Bicentennial, MIT has carried out studies of several social and intellectual aspects of the world we inhabit at the beginning of our third century. Our objective has been to inquire how human beings might deal more intelligently and humanely with these factors, most of which are closely linked to developments in science and technology.

The papers prepared for these inquiries are being published in an MIT Bicentennial Studies Series of which this volume is a part. Other studies in the series deal with the social impact of the telephone, the future of computing and information processing, linguistics and cognitive psychology, the economics of the new international economic order, and administrative and economic factors in air pollution.

It is our hope that these volumes will be of interest and value to those concerned now with these questions and, additionally, might provide useful historical perspective to those concerned with the same or similar questions on the occasion of the U.S. Tricentennial.

Jerome B. Wiesner
President

Preface

The papers in this volume were given as lectures at the Massachusetts Institute of Technology during the winter and spring of 1976–1977. The lecture series was planned and organized by a committee whose members were Manson Benedict, Jagdish N. Bhagwati, Lincoln P. Bloomfield, John M. Deutch, Bernard T. Feld, Ted R. I. Greenwood, Amelia C. Leiss, George W. Rathjens, Walter A. Rosenblith, Jack P. Ruina, Eugene B. Skolnikoff, Leon Trilling, and Norman C. Dahl, Chairman. We are indebted to this committee and to Lord Solly Zuckerman who gave most valuable assistance during the planning phase. We thank Elizabeth Frink for her design of an appropriate and beautiful medal, copies of which were struck and presented to the lecturers to commemorate their participation in this bicentennial lecture series. Our thanks also go to Merriam B. Bourscaren for her great help in carrying out the series.

The letter of invitation to each lecturer was accompanied by a background paper which is reproduced in this volume. This paper discusses various aspects of change and security in today's world and suggests a broad framework in which the lecturers might organize their individual approaches to the problems of change and security.

The introduction gives an overview of the major ideas presented in the lectures, organized along the order of the discussion in the background paper. Ideas related to a specific aspect of security are grouped so that the views of different lectures can be compared. The lectures are arranged in the order in which they were given.

Our deep appreciation is extended to the lecturers. Their thoughtful contributions made the lecture series a fitting part of the U.S. Bicentennial celebration.

N.C.D.
J.B.W.

Contributors

Roy Jenkins, President of the Commission of the European Communities

Willy Brandt, Chairman, Social Democratic Party of Germany; President, the Socialist International

McGeorge Bundy, President, Ford Foundation

David A. Hamburg, President, Institute of Medicine of the U.S. National Academy of Sciences

Sigvard Eklund, Director General, International Atomic Energy Agency

Roberto de Oliveira Campos, Brazilian Ambassador to Great Britain

Georgi A. Arbatov, Director, Institute of U.S. and Canadian Studies of the Academy of Sciences of the USSR

Canon Burgess Carr, General Secretary, All Africa Conference of Churches

Robert S. McNamara, President, World Bank

Frank Church, United States Senator

Background Paper

The international political situation is balanced precariously today because of a relatively new and complex set of political, economic, social, and military forces existing within and between countries. Although some of these forces have historical antecedents predating World War II, most have derived from world developments since 1945, prominent among which have been the quest for political independence, with a consequent upsurge of nationalism; the pervasive aspiration for higher standards of living, with a consequent awareness of the increasing gap between the poor and the rich nations; and the explosive advances in science and technology, with a consequent infusion of change into almost all aspects of life and all parts of the world, one of the most significant changes being the current dependence on nuclear weapons and missile delivery systems.

These forces have created wholly new conditions within and between nations. The formation of a large number of independent nations has upset old relationships, and new ones which offer mutually acceptable benefits and costs have not yet emerged. The aspirations for better living conditions have not been satisfied and this has generated political tensions both within countries and between the poor and the rich countries. The advances in science and technology have brought major alterations in economic, political, and military affairs, and, concurrently, they have expanded greatly the information and perceptions available to societies, affecting deep-seated patterns of culture, behavior, and expectations.

Since these transformations have occurred within little more than the working life of a single generation, it is not surprising that the world has been unable to digest and adjust to the consequent changes. Man has long known that he and his institutions must accommodate to change, but our past experience has not prepared us to accommodate to such rapid change. What is new in the present situation is that the exploitation of science and technology has so accelerated the *rate* of change of man's condition that our traditional means for dealing with political, economic, social, and military change are no longer adequate to the task. The need is not only to cope with our present problems but to develop capability to accommodate rapidly and without violence to continuing change created by man's own actions.

To stimulate thought about practical initiatives which nations might take, individually and collectively, to gain better control of our more dynamic world, MIT has undertaken to sponsor a lecture series in which world leaders from several countries will address the question of World Change and World Security. Because of the position MIT occupies in relation to science and technology, abroad as well as in the United States, it has a particular responsibility to concern itself with this question of how man might better respond to a world in which change has become rapid and pervasive as a result of the growing technological base of society.

Organization of the Lecture Series

Several world political and intellectual leaders are being invited to prepare lectures for the series, each dealing with such specific aspects of world security as he chooses. The lectures will be delivered to evening audiences at MIT over a period of weeks during the winter and spring of 1976-1977. Following completion of the series, the MIT Press will publish the lectures in a volume.

Since the lecturers will come from a spectrum of experience and national settings, it is anticipated that collectively they will deal with a variety of aspects of change and security. This is to be expected since neither change nor security has simple dimensions. It is suggested that the lecturers' approaches need be similar only in the time frame in which they deal with the question of world security, generally proceeding as follows:

Take as background what you consider to be significant forces and critical situations now existing within and between nations and your views of the most likely changes that might develop or be brought about in these during the next two decades. In that context, and in reference to the specific aspects of security you are considering, outline policies you believe should and could be pursued by particular nations or groups of nations to increase both their individual security and the overall security of the world community during these two decades.

From the discussion in the introduction it is evident that the word "security" is meant to imply more than the traditional concept of military defense of the territory and population of a nation-state and its allies. Indeed, the lecture series has been organized on the premise that the world lacks concepts of security capable of coping with the range of dangers now facing mankind. In effect, the lecturers are being asked to discuss security in a context which takes account of political, economic, and social factors as well as military factors. This is no easy assignment. At the same time there is no more urgent task than to generate ideas which, by virtue of their political insight and intellectual content, will stimulate widespread discussion of practical steps man might take to alter his attitudes, his methods and his institutions for dealing with various aspects of change and security in the modern world.

Some Aspects of Change and Security

With no intention to constrain the lecturers, the organizers have identified a limited number of aspects of change and security which they expect will be among those treated by at least some of the lecturers. These aspects are discussed below and the brief remarks under each aspect give a view of what the organizers perceive to be major dimensions of each. The intention of these remarks is to suggest to lecturers discussing a specific aspect a common point of departure, with which they may proceed to agree or disagree, so those who attend the lectures and those who later read them will be better able to relate the views of one lecturer to those of another. This background paper will be distributed to audiences attending the lectures and included in the introduction to the published volume of lectures.

The group of aspects discussed below begins with broad social aspects and ends with aspects related to current military questions. Although a premise of the organizers is that military power no longer provides a shield against most of the dangers facing the world, unless nuclear war power can be controlled in the short run, we may not have the opportunity to evolve for the long run a system of security which provides protection against other dangers as well as military power. At the same time, unless we have a concept of possible long-run security needs we will be handicapped in judging among alternative short-term security policies. As always, we need a vision of where we want to go, but we also need practical means for traversing the intervening years.

North-South Relations

One of the most intractable problems of the current world is how to close the gulf between the prosperity of the developed countries and the poverty of the less developed countries. Although the average growth rate of the less developed countries in the 1950s and 1960s was unprecedented in world history because it was at such a much higher level than their growth rate during the decades previous to World War II, the net result of these years was still a widening of the gap between them and the developed countries. Aside from any humanitarian concerns, it can be argued that this gap needs to be closed for pragmatic interests of the developed countries. Just as the less developed countries need the goods and services of the developed countries, the latter need trade with the less developed countries. The complex economies of the developed countries require import of many key raw materials, and this injects a genuine element of interdependence into the relations between the developed and the less developed countries.

It is unlikely that there will be stability in north-south relations as long as the present gap in living standards persists, and thus it would seem that the long-term security interests of the entire world depend in fair measure upon relatively rapid narrowing of this gap. But practical means by which this can be carried out are not clear. The developed countries have a dynamism which, unless checked by resource or other constraints, is likely to carry them to continued growth at somewhere near current rates. On the other hand, the experience of the past two decades makes clear that there is no obvious or certain road to economic and political development for the less developed countries and that they face tough political and economic problems in their efforts to bring about rapid growth. Thus, rapid narrowing of the gap in living standards very likely will require other actions in addition to increasing the growth rates of the less developed countries, and one of the central issues of north-south relations is the pressure of the less developed countries for actions that will permit them to share the benefits of total world economic growth. A further complicating factor is that for many aspects of interdependence the power gap is as important as the wealth gap , as is evidence by increasing demands of the less developed countries for a more significant role in the decision-making processes that affect their interest. What are ways in which this imbalance in the human condition can be reduced substantially over the next few decades?

East-West Relations

Stable security arrangements between the western-style democracies (the OECD countries) and the Soviet Union and the People's Republic of China are central to any world security system. All three elements of this triad are having internal problems which require much of their attention and energy. The democratic governments have increasingly accepted responsibility for the domestic economy as a whole and for various group services within it (such as welfare) until many find themselves overextended and unable to discharge all the responsibilities expected of them and, in some cases, are faced with a crisis of confidence in government and governmental institutions. In the Soviet Union the leadership is confronted with serious structural problems in agriculture, in productivity, and in industrial applications of advanced technology, as well as with increasing pressures for consumer goods. China is going through the change in leadership from Mao Tse-tung and, based on the experience of the past few years, the future course of events there is unpredictable. Given these conditions what sort of security policies over the next two decades are likely to give these nations freedom to cope with their internal problems, restrain each other's expansion of hegemony, and yet possibly lay the base for a more stable international security system over the longer run?

Resource Constraints

In a long time frame the availability of raw materials and the resources of the biosphere are a significant aspect of security. For some material resources, oil for example, "long" is only of the order of a century and therefore the problem of physical nonavailability will soon be before us. Material resources may also become nonavailable unexpectedly because of political decisions, as was demonstrated by the OPEC crisis. As the level of industrialization of the rest of the world draws closer to that of the developed countries, questions of material resource constraint will become increasingly pressing. These questions will be exacerbated if the world population continues to grow at its present rate, both because of the increased rates of depletion and because of political problems generated by increased demands on the resources. While science and technology may be able to provide replacement or substitution for many resources, the scale of needed human, technological, and financial investment may be beyond the capability of individual nations and require multilateral efforts, further increasing interdependence.

The resources of the biosphere are in even more need of collaborative effort between nations to secure their continued quality and availability.

Population growth is significant here also, not only for the increased demands for food but for the increased pressure on many aspects of the biosphere. The dangers of polluting the atmosphere or the waters of the earth,
either purposefully or inadvertently, are well known. But there are also
possibilities that resources will become unavailable for reasons entirely beyond the control of man and that an international collaborative effort
would offer the only hope of alleviation. The most real of these is the possibility that the general climate of the world will repeat past patterns and
enter into a cooler period over the coming decades, with consequent major
reductions in the agricultural production in northern regions and some
monsoon areas. Although yet only speculative and not a probability despite trends toward reduced harvests in the U.S.S.R. and Canada, such a
course of events would produce widespread trauma in a world unprepared
to collaborate to respond to such a situation. Thus, on several counts it
would appear that the protection and general availability of raw materials
and the resources of the biosphere will be increasingly important political
objectives of national and global security.

Institutional Constraints
An apparent characteristic of many governmental institutions today is
their inability to cope with the problems they are charged to handle. One
student of government has characterized this as "the governability of complexity" while a former head of government has characterized the problems of a democracy as the complexity of social issues, the difficulty of
dealing with complicated international relationships, the ease with which
public opinion can be manipulated, and the increasing difficulty in controlling legislative and bureaucratic actions. To judge by remarks at the 25th
Party Congress in March, the Soviet institutions are having similar problems in discharging their responsibilities , indicating that institutional difficulties may be common across both ideological and physical boundaries.
If anything, the difficulties appear to be more acute at the international
institutional level.

When a situation requires multinational agreement, it is necessary to
have intelligent and effective bureaucratic action at both national and international levels in order to negotiate security arrangements and to ad-
minister their execution. Given this need, development of practical ways
to improve the structure and functioning of institutions seems to be a matter of highest priority for a world security system capable of accommodating to continuing change rapidly and without violence. In this
connection it is natural to ask whether it is possible to transform the

United Nations system into an effective mechanism for coping with change and maintaining stability. If so, what actions would be required to achieve this transformation? If not, in what other directions should efforts be made to develop and strengthen international institutional capabilities?

U.S.-U.S.S.R. Strategic Nuclear Capabilities

The question of U.S.-U.S.S.R. nuclear equivalence or parity has dominated world security thinking since World War II. Given the present capabilities of both sides, what are the military and political considerations that argue for a continuation of this focus? Does it matter any more just how large the U.S. and the U.S.S.R. strategic forces are or how they are composed? Is there room for significant asymmetries in capability or reductions below the current levels of nuclear forces? For what security situations are nuclear weapons effective instruments of policy? For what situation are they ineffective?

These are some of the larger issues that underlie the U.S.-U.S.S.R. bilateral negotiations which focus on specific aspects of force levels, kinds of weapons and verification of compliance to agreements. These bilateral negotiations are accompanied by intense negotiations within each country among powerful groups which have differing goals as to what should be achieved out of the bilateral negotiations, and here the arguments are often made in relation to the question of U.S.S.R. (or U.S.) hegemony aspirations and to concepts such as "mutual deterrence," "sufficiency," "second-strike capability," and "flexible response."

Given the reality of the present situation, which has elements of stability but also the potential of catastrophe if things do break down, what other options are available for dealing with the nuclear danger as the world moves through the coming decades of change? In this context, what are practical means for dealing with the question of proliferation of nuclear weapons?

The Escalation of Violence

Although the world has avoided the use of nuclear weapons since World War II, armed conflict has persisted. Interstate wars and civil wars have been fought with conventional weapons, and individuals or small groups have used such weapons to terrorize other individuals or groups in attempts to coerce them or, through them, their governments. This violence has made tension and uncertainty a daily fact of life in many parts of the world, often intensified by limitations on freedom of speech or movement or by activities of a national intelligence and police apparatus imposed by

government in the name of national security. Furthermore, the sophistica-
tion of conventional weapons continues to increase as a result of energetic
weapons research and development programs in several countries, thereby
increasing their capability to inflict loss of life and physical damage, and a
flourishing international trade in arms has rapidly proliferated this destructive capacity throughout the world, with much of the arms going into regions where tensions between neighboring states are high. The future is
made more ominous by the potential for the proliferation of nuclear
weaponry.

Many questions arise. Are there institutions that can be strengthened, or
new ones invented, which will lessen man's reliance on violence to protect
his rights and redress his grievances? Can nations—both sellers and buyers—
be led to reassess the costs and benefits of the international trade in arms?
Can nations find ways to make international terrorism unappealing to non-
national groups as a way of pressing their claims? Can the human, institutional, and physical resources that now are expended so freely on real or
potential international violence be directed to the amelioration of other
pressing human needs? These questions have no ready answers, but they
are central to the question of world security for the coming decades.

September 1976

Introduction

The objective of the Lecture Series on World Change and World Security was to stimulate wide discussion of practical steps man might take to alter his attitudes, his methods, and his institutions for dealing with various aspects of change and security in the modern world. Lecturers from a variety of national and international settings and professional backgrounds were invited so that the issues of change and security could be examined from many directions. The diverse and remarkably qualified lecturers who participated in the series have indeed provided a number of analyses and ideas that should contribute substantially to a better understanding of many aspects of change and security in today's and tomorrow's world.

Given the terms of reference suggested in the background paper, it is not surprising that the same issues appear repeatedly in these lectures. But it also is clear that the lecturers do share a consensus on what are the most critical aspects of change and security, even though they view the issues from quite different vantage points. In this introduction we have brought these differing perspectives together in what we hope will be a useful guide to the reader, following roughly the order of discussion in the background paper.

The lecturers are in agreement with the background paper thesis that the exploitation of science and technology has so accelerated the *rate* of change of man's condition that our traditional means for dealing with political, social, and military change are no longer adequate to the task. Georgi Arbatov observes that anxiety about the influence of accelerated scientific and technological progress probably is due to the fact that this influence has been of a very contradictory nature. For example, an excessively large proportion of the scientific and technological effort has been concentrated on the arms race, while the tremendous achievements of our technological civilization have had little effect on many of the fundamental problems confronting humanity. Arbatov sees no reason to expect that future changes which science and technology make in society automatically will eliminate such contradictions and acquire "a purely positive character." At the same time he thinks the past two decades have been fruitful in that our societies have gained a better comprehension of problems facing mankind and are beginning to give serious thought to ways to deal with them.

Willy Brandt reviews the changes in world conditions since World War II and makes the point that at the beginning there was little appreciation that we were entering an age of upheaval. We neither realized how much the industrial societies would be pressed by new problems nor anticipated the scope of changes that would be brought about by developments in the countries of the Third World. Brandt cautions that we cannot expect the rate of change to decrease much. He predicts that for the foreseeable future the world will continue to be faced with more problems than it can solve quickly enough; the realistic political objective must be to keep this dangerous disparity within the narrowest possible limits. To accomplish this, Brandt says we must improve our political systems to provide capacities for long-range analysis and for political groupings guided by ideas and not only focused on competition for power.

David Hamburg notes that the world we live in is mainly one that we have made for ourselves only very recently on the evolutionary time scale, and so the problems that concern us today are mostly the product of man's own activities over the few centuries since the industrial revolution. We do not know how well we are suited biologically for the world we now live in, for there were millions of years of human evolution and natural selection that shaped our ancestors in ways that suited their earlier environments. Hamburg believes we must try to understand the forces that molded our species in the past in order to be able to choose among future options for change.

With respect to specific dangers that threaten world security, many of the lecturers put emphasis on the problems of the developing countries and the current confrontation of ideas about a new international economic order. Roberto Campos finds fault on both sides in the controversy over the new international economic order. He asserts that developing countries evade critical problems by blaming external influences for internal inequities even as they neglect to reduce these inequities by pursuing internal reforms in such areas as agricultural policy, land tenure, fiscal policy, and population planning. Campos accuses the industrialized countries of indulging in institutionalized hypocrisy in some of their relations with the poor developing countries. As one example he cites the paying of lip service to liberal trade policies while adopting protectionist measures against agricultural products and low-technology manufactured goods from developing countries. As another example he asserts that the industrialized countries speak in support of political and economic interdependence yet refuse to share meaningful decision-making with the developing countries, particularly in matters concerned with the international monetary system. Campos makes the point that the demand for a new international economic order is part of a long-term movement, and rich nations must recognize that development of the poor nations is an essential element for their own sustained development. In the economic field this will require, among other changes, that industrialized countries make internal adjustments to provide for diversified imports from developing countries. Politically, the industrialized countries must learn to accept different ideological preferences and political systems in the developing countries. Campos observes that the great majority of developing countries have some form of authoritarian political system and suggests that, for coping with their problems, some form of "liberal-authoritarian" system may be more relevant than importing Western patterns of democratic organization.

The demands of the developing countries for a more just ordering of the world economy cannot be evaded, asserts Willy Brandt, since there cannot be a lasting and secure coexistence of affluence and misery. The developed countries will have to make up their minds in good time to transfer resources to the Third World, for history demonstrates that it never makes sense to try to hold "overdue bastions" with a last great summoning of strength. At the same time the developing countries will have to forego actions that might endanger the economic cycle in the industrialized world. Brandt also points out that the industrialized states under communist rule must share responsibility for aiding the developing countries and should prepare to participate in international discussions and negotiations on raw materials, trade, and development aid.

Burgess Carr focuses on the development problems of Africa. He asserts that, in the largely nonviolent devolution of colonial power, conditions were set up that have frustrated the new African nations in consolidating their political independence and achieving social transformation of their societies. One such condition was that the territorial boundaries, political structures, and institutions of the new nations did not allow for the social and political traditions indigenous to Africa. Another was the determination of the colonial powers to keep the new nations within the orbit of their capitalist world by creating a group of Africans who would identify with the interests of the colonialists. According to Carr the colonists corrupted this group by providing them opportunity to amass instant, ill-gotten wealth, and this process initiated the pervasive corruption that debilitates many African states today. Carr describes a unique linguistic, ecological, political, religious, and aesthetic African cultural identity which he feels can form the basis of indigenous political institutions more appropriate and effective than those that resulted from decolonization. He expects these institutions will provide greater regard for the group rights of society as a whole as against the private rights of individuals, reflecting the communalistic basis of traditional African society. Carr sees this transformation and the elimination of colonialism from southern Africa as the tasks of highest priority for Africa in the coming decades.

Sigvard Eklund calls attention to the fact that necessary improvements in living conditions in the developing countries will create increasing energy demands for intensified agricultural production and industrialization. He points out that the oil crisis has shown that a shortage of energy or a sharp rise in its price affects developing countries hardest. While an affluent country can conserve on its energy use with only marginal ill effects, in a poor country energy conservation is another term for hardship.

Georgi Arbatov takes the position that the developing countries cannot solve their problems without radical economic and sociopolitical changes. He says this is necessary because during the colonial period the majority of developing countries were molded into agricultural and raw material-providing appendages to the industrial countries, and they have not escaped from these Western-dominated economic relations that are unsuited to their development needs. Although Arbatov asserts that the optimal road of development is the noncapitalist road he says that in the spirit of détente the capitalist and socialist developed countries can join efforts to assist the Third World to solve important problems of development. He cites stopping arms sales to the developing countries as one area where joint action by the industrialized countries could free large sums of badly needed money for development purposes.

In his analysis of the population problem Robert McNamara points out that if current trends in fertility rates continue, the world's population will stabilize near the year 2100 at about eleven billion people, nine out of ten of whom will live in today's developing countries. With this population the levels of poverty, stress, and frustration in the developing countries inevitably will create social, political, and military instability. But McNamara says a world of eleven billion is not inevitable, since recent studies make it appear likely that reductions in fertility in developing countries can be brought about by specific kinds of socioeconomic development. This opportunity to avoid such a crowded and unstable world gives all countries of the world a common stake in speeding socioeconomic gains in the developing countries.

Looking at East-West relations and comparing Europe today with the conditions of fifteen or twenty years ago, Brandt finds peace somewhat less endangered. Although he does not expect differences in ideologies and political systems between East and West to be eliminated, he sees no reasonable alternative to a strong policy of détente. Brandt views détente as a matter of making peace more secure by negotiating about concrete problems where a common denominator can be found, however much the political orders are opposed to one another. In respect to military forces in Europe and the Mutual Balanced Force Reductions negotiations in Vienna, Brandt believes that the aim of détente policy should be to bring about, step by step, a situation in which a military attack without prior buildup will be virtually impossible. Brandt thinks the Helsinki Conference on Security and Cooperation in Europe was a step forward for human rights even though it aroused hopes in many people of the East and West which, for the time being, cannot be met by the European reality. Admitting there were deficiencies in the conference and its texts, Brandt faults the United States for failing to understand the significance of the fact that East and West did agree on important declarations of intent and guidelines for relations.

Roy Jenkins also sees the Helsinki Declaration as an important document of hope for Europeans. In his position as President of the Commission of the European Communities, Jenkins is much concerned with East-West relations. Jenkins feels that the community can contribute more than the sum of its parts to the resolution of these economic, political, and military relations if the member states can rise above their various national problems and difficulties to negotiate and act with one will. He sees the whole North Atlantic area as the proper unit for defense of Europe and foresees the eventual needs for the European states to integrate their own defense industries and standardize equipment among themselves and the United States.

McGeorge Bundy notes that relations of the United States with the Soviet Union have been a persistent and absorbing issue in the United States over the past two generations. Polarities of optimism and pessimism about Soviet actions and intentions have heightened debates on such questions as Yalta, the Cold War, liberation in Eastern Europe, atmospheric testing, Communist Cuba, the antiballistic missile, and, more recently, the scale and meaning of Soviet rearmament. Bundy makes the point that, except for the period running roughly from the Truman Doctrine in 1947 through the ascendancy of Foster Dulles in the late 1950s, the approaches of the government as well as the desire of the public have been dual. There have been efforts to find agreements with the Soviet Union as well as efforts to contain Soviet pressures that were felt to be illegitimate or dangerous. Bundy thinks this duality will continue because the American public is capable of living with the apparently conflicting propositions that the United States is in opposition to many things the Soviet Union either does or would like to do, and, at the same time, that U.S. and Soviet societies, if they are to survive at all, must survive together. Bundy also calls attention to the fact that the political and technical analyses of U.S.–Soviet issues have become much less simple as more has been learned about them and that it is essential to have first class people and institutions making these analyses.

Referring mainly to the Soviet-American armament competition, Georgi Arbatov observes that in spite of relaxation of tensions in the political sphere and some advantageous cooperation it has not been possible to stem the arms race. Arbatov attributes responsibility for this failure to the West. He says that the economic system of the West has permitted the subordination of policy making to the interests of the military-industrial complex. An additional influence, he says, has been the heritage of the cold war in political thinking, which has made it possible to play on false or invented fears and thereby to secure support for dangerous and irrational decisions. Arbatov states that this situation in which the arms race persists despite improvement of Soviet-American relations is dangerous because it can foil or inhibit political détente and thus further intensify the arms race. He also points out that if current growth rates of military expenditures continue into the future, the amounts spent on armaments may jeopardize the economies of many countries, including that of the United States.

Roberto Campos expects the East-West ideological confrontation to continue for some time despite efforts at détente. He bases this prediction on what he observes to be differences in motivation between East and West and a degree of asymmetry of behavior resulting from the fact that the West preaches ideological pluralism and the East practices ideological rigidity. Tracing the development of East-West power relationships, Campos describes these as having evolved from a short-lived American nuclear monopoly immediately after World War II to strategic bipolarity in the 1950s and gradually during the 1960s to a balance of power scenario within both the socialist and the Western camps. Today Campos sees a world balance of power among the United States, the Soviet Union, the People's Republic of China, the European Community, and Japan, a balance facing challenges from several sources. One challenge comes from rising regional powers such as Brazil, Iran, India, Australia, and perhaps Nigeria. Another comes from the major redistribution of financial power and liquidity brought about by the OPEC cartel. And a challenge comes from the increasing assertiveness of the developing countries' claims for a more genuinely multilateral mechanism of decision-making and for the establishment of a new international economic order.

Resource constraints are seen as a critical factor in future security. In his lecture Sigvard Eklund concentrates on the energy resources of the world. He predicts that if world population continues to increase as expected and if per capita energy consumption grows at a rate needed to bring substantial improvements of living standards in the developing countries within the coming fifty years, then the known fossil fuel resources of the world will be exhausted by the end of the next century unless other major sources of energy become available soon. Eklund thinks there are only three other possible sources of major energy supply: nuclear fission, nuclear fusion, and solar-related energy (solar, wind, tidal, ocean gradient, etc.). He notes that although the feasibility of nuclear fission power was demonstrated some thirty-five years ago, the complexity and cost of developing the process have been such that today it accounts for only about 10 percent of electricity production in the industrialized countries. Given this experience and the fact that feasibility of nuclear fusion and solar-related energy have yet to be demonstrated, Eklund concludes that for several decades nuclear fission will be the only additional major energy source available. But Eklund then states that the world's proven uranium reserves used in today's fission power reactors will produce power equivalent only to about one-quarter of that available from known oil and gas reserves and, as a consequence, current fission technology does not offer sufficient relief. He says this leaves no alternative but rapid development and deployment of the fast breeder fission reactor which would multiply the energy available from uranium by a factor of 100 to 1000. Eklund urges that a full-scale breeder reactor be developed collaboratively by the nuclear supplier nations and that an international undertaking should be started for fuel manufacture, reprocessing of spent fuel and recycling of plutonium, and waste disposal. He recognizes that a large, worldwide nuclear power program will entail dangers from nuclear waste disposal and possible diversion of nuclear materials for weapons use but believes the disposal problem can be solved technically and that universal adherence to the International

Atomic Energy Agency's safeguards program of inspection and verification will make materials diversion difficult and unlikely.

Frank Church also addresses the question of nuclear energy. He concentrates on the decision of the Carter administration to defer indefinitely nuclear fuel reprocessing and to halt development of the breeder reactor in an attempt to avoid entering the plutonium stage of nuclear power generation. The administration feels that widespread use of plutonium-based breeder reactors will create unacceptable risks of proliferation of nuclear weapons. Church asserts that this unilateral renunciation of breeder reactors coupled with an offer to other countries of a guaranteed supply of enriched uranium to fuel their conventional reactors will not achieve the administration's goal of including other countries to forego development of the breeder reactor. He explains that most other countries have limited energy resources, and they will not give up the breeder reactor because it offers them the possibility of eventual energy independence. Church says the energy-deficient countries were traumatized by the 600 percent oil price increase mandated by the OPEC cartel and understandably are unwilling to exchange dependence on foreign oil for dependence on foreign natural uranium, which they may see as being unsure in long-term supply and subject to drastic price manipulation. He urges that the United States continue development of the breeder reactor and work toward the goal of eventual international ownership and control of the fuel cycle necessary to sustain commercial reactors in all nonweapons states. Church believes that with a system of international ownership under the auspices of the International Atomic Energy Agency it will be possible to devise effective operational safeguards against proliferation.

Touching only briefly on the problem of resources, Georgi Arbatov emphasizes the need for international scientific and technical collaboration on resource problems, saying that in the long perspective scientific and technical progress alone can offer a way out of the difficulties created by raw material shortages.

The requirement for new institutional forms to cope with changing world conditions is clearly much on the minds of the lecturers. Roy Jenkins deals extensively with the development of the institutions of the European Community. He notes that this effort, which is essentially a political enterprise, has been pursued by largely economic means. This was because it proved easier to form the iron and steel community and the European economic community than to make a European defense community or a European political community. Jenkins says that although the European Community in its various aspects now has economic, political, and judicial reality, it is very far from complete and faces serious problems. At the same time he makes the point that the European nations depend for their strength on each other, and this provides a certain logic driving the community members toward political cooperation and perhaps one day to a full European political community.

Willy Brandt observes that the political systems of the Western democracies are relatively efficient repair mechanisms but are not geared for early diagnosis. He feels there is a great challenge to develop democratic institutions capable of analyzing and dealing with major problems without creating freedom-stifling bureaucracies, whether governmental or nongovernmental. He also agrees that many of the problems facing countries are too complex to be coped with by one nation and says this leaves no option but to develop new forms of frontier-crossing cooperation instead of thinking only in terms of national sovereignty.

Frank Church observes that the nuclear weapons proliferation dilemma presents a classic case study of technological advance outpacing our political capacity to deal with the technology. He proposes new institutional arrangements to deal with the problem, namely international ownership and control of the fuel cycle under the auspices of the International Atomic Energy Agency (IAEA). Sigvard Eklund points out that the IAEA safeguards system represents the first time in history that an international inspection system has been accepted. Eklund says that much experience has been gained in operating the system and while there is room for improvement the system works well. He suggests it might serve as an institutional model for other similar tasks in the realm of disarmament.

The strategic nuclear capabilities of the U.S. and the U.S.S.R. are discussed by Georgi Arbatov who says that the growth of American and Soviet strategic nuclear weapons has given the threat of war a new dimension: it has turned the threat of war into an issue of human survival. It is the realization of this fact, he says, that has roused the powerful forces of self-preservation which form the basis of the policy of détente. Arbatov sees the past two decades of nuclear confrontation as a period of dangerous mistakes and mounting threats and also a period of first initiatives to forestall these threats. In these decades the development of strategic nuclear weapons on both sides was based on the concept of deterrence, on having the capability to inflict an unacceptable level of damage on the other side should that side initiate nuclear war. Arbatov disclaims deterrence as an ideal strategy and observes that it led to enormous redundancy in weapons, but he makes the point that it did create a strategic impasse which so far has helped to avoid a nuclear conflict. He sees recent and cur-

rent weapons development as being destablizing, although he notes that
the Soviet-American agreement on the ABM (antiballistic missile) did stop
one destabilizing system. Arbatov says that United States introduction of
the MIRV (multiple, independently targeted, re-entry vehicle) system was
destabilizing because it introduced an increase in the number of nuclear
warheads that greatly exceeded the requirements of deterrence. In
Arbatov's view the availability of these "redundant" warheads led to rein-
troduction, at a new and more dangerous level, of the idea of counterforce
employment of strategic weapons. He also thinks the cruise missile will be
destabilizing for the reason that it will be difficult or even impossible to
conclude arms agreements including them because of the formidable problems of verifying compliance. Arbatov further makes the point that science
and technology related to weapons are making such strides that one cannot rule out the emergency of unforeseen dangers. In his view these trends
increase the risk of a possible acute international crisis leading to a tragic
and irrevocable error even though neither government wants nuclear war.
Also, the failure of the United States and the Soviet Union to control their
arms race creates a general situation which makes the proliferation of nuclear weapons more probable. Arbatov observes that both sides agree that
the first step in curbing the strategic arms race should be to conclude a
SALT II treaty, but they disagree as to whether it should be based on the
Vladivostok accord. In Arbatov's view, taking account of all the complexities of the strategic balance that imply a number of essential asymmetries,
the SALT II treaty must be based on what was agreed on in Vladivostok
and the negotiations that followed it. If a SALT II treaty can be concluded,
Arbatov sees the possibility of moving on to discussion about how to start
the reduction of mass annihilation weapons and perhaps even about a ban
on new types of weapons systems. Arbatov suggests that our difficulty in
dealing with the arms race stems partly from the fact that the capacities
and art of policy making lag sadly behind weapons science and technology,
that the political instruments and methods used to exercise control over
science and technology have remained to a large extent in the "prenuclear"
stage. He says that during the next two decades there will be mounting
pressure to adapt existing sociopolitical realities to the present level of
scientific and technological potentialities.

   The manner in which the United States has arrived at decision and action
in respect to the Soviet Union is the subject of McGeorge Bundy's lecture.
He observes that the two societies necessarily are concerned, often preoccupied, with one another because each knows that nuclear weapons give
the other an obvious capacity to make the future unendurable for itself

and for many others. The relationship has not been a simple one at any time on either side. Bundy feels that on the U.S. side, through most of the postwar period, decisions have been arrived at from two different starting points, one of hope and one of fear, sometimes one of hope inspired of fear. Occasionally debate on an issue has occurred at the time of decision, but most often it has been prospective or retrospective. Bundy suggests this has been the case because crises and agreements with the Soviet Union have tended to focus both authority and support on the president. Whether the decision be for confrontation or agreement, even in an unpleasant crisis, the immediate reaction has tended to be to look to the White House. Bundy says this has happened because the decisions have brought out in their support, and successfully in their support, the public opinion that resists Soviet pressure on the one hand and welcomes reasonable agreement on the other. He sees this as the reason why, although there have been struggles over getting the necessary Senate majority of votes for arms control treaties, these struggles have not been as hard as the negotiators initially thought they would be. Bundy's view is that Senate debate has not constricted decisions with respect to the Soviet Union because in the field of decision, as distinct from the field of debate, the initiative lies with the executive branch if it takes it. But this initiative is constrained by two realities of American public opinion: that there must be a real answer to any Soviet threat to U.S. security and that there must be good agreements. The executive branch has to pay attention at all times, before as well as during the moment of decision, to the question of public confidence in its double attitude of hope and fear. A crisis to be survived will require a solid basis of good efforts to avoid it, and an agreement to be approved will require a strong basis of confidence that it does not endanger security. Bundy points out, however, that the complexity of nuclear warfare makes it very hard to bring about public understanding of the issues. As an example, he says that the public discussion on the cruise missile has yet not come near to laying a base for national accord on whatever decision the government makes about this weapon. What is needed, Bundy says, is analysis that will provide understanding of both the technical and political issues so public discussion can be an informed debate.

Roberto Campos observes that what might be called the "positive power" of the United States and the Soviet Union has decreased with the advent of nuclear weapons. The nuclear impasse has limited their capability to intervene, and this has eroded the traditional linkage between power and order. Campos says this erosion has been one of the factors enabling the developing countries to use their "negative power" of challenging the existing economic order and existing international and institutional arrangements.

David Hamburg asks whether we have perceived that the danger of human extinction requires the cooperation of our mutually suspicious societies to achieve the superordinate goal of elimination of nuclear weapons. He notes that we have lived in the shadow of this danger for three decades, but world leaders still tend to speak in nineteenth-century terms. He also says that most individuals and small groups feel a sense of helplessness in the face of such dangers and tend automatically to avoid thinking about them. Hamburg thinks it is not yet clear whether we have come to this perception, suggesting that the time interval may have been too short for such an appraisal.

Two lecturers spoke of violence. Burgess Carr rejects limiting the concept of violence to the response oppressed people make in the face of massive repression and dehumanization, saying there is structural violence in racial and colonial oppression as well as social violence in economic, class, and political exploitation. Carr also suggests that violence can be redemptive in special situations if it is used selectively, not for revenge and vengeance but as a means of liberating both the oppressed and their oppressors. But he says Africans are committed to eliminating violence—they are tired of oppression and plunder and yearn for peace.

Pointing up the difficulty of bringing about change in man's violent behavior, David Hamburg observes that much of human aggression is in the service of human attachment. He notes that we kill our enemies and ravage the planet in the commitment to those we care about. In the name of love and duty and brotherhood, Hamburg says, we carry out the threats and attacks that now constitute the ultimate peril to our species.

Robert McNamara's lecture analyzes the population problem. Short of thermonuclear war itself, McNamara sees rampant population growth as the gravest security threat the world faces in the decades immediately ahead. At the beginning of the nineteenth century the world population reached a total of one billion after more than a million years of growth. Yet it took only 120 years to add the second billion, thirty-two years to add the third billion, and fifteen years more to reach today's total of four billion. At the current global rate of 2 percent increase per year the fifth billion will be added in about eleven years. What happens beyond this point depends upon how quickly the birth rates are brought down throughout the world. For example, if the current trend in declining birth rate continues, the world population will begin to stabilize about the year 2020 and will reach a steady-state level of eleven billion some seventy

years later. But if birth rates were to decline more quickly so that the stabilization begins in 2000 (instead of 2020), the ultimate population would
be about eight billion, or only twice today's population. McNamara believes it imperative that the world hold its population to this level of eight
billion. He also believes it is possible. Analysis of the population history of
the industrialized countries shows that a demographic transition from high
to low birth rates has occurred as development proceeded. In order to
keep the world population from going beyond eight billion it will be necessary to speed up the transition from high to low birth rates in the developing world. McNamara says that two aspects of recent population trends
suggest it will be possible to accomplish this. First, it appears that birth
rates in the developing world have at least begun to turn downward, although not yet by nearly the amount needed to keep the ultimate total
within the eight billion figure. Second, an analysis of population growth
and natural development programs in a number of developing countries
indicates that the drop in the birth rate can be accelerated by giving priority to certain key factors in the development plan of a country. The
factors most closely linked to fertility decline appear to be health, education, broadly distributed economic growth, urbanization, and, above all
else, the enhanced status of women. If the developing countries give these
factors strong support in their development programs and also provide
parents with a broad choice of contraceptive techniques and services,
McNamara thinks the developing world will be able to achieve the needed
speed-up in the demographic transition from high to low birth rates. But
he warns that quick action is necessary.

David Hamburg's lecture looks at change and security from the perspective of human evolution. He sees reasons for both hope and despair about
the future of the human species. While pointing out that clues to the past
are scanty and elusive, he says that conclusions drawn from evolutionary
research on behavior can be tested by observation on nonhuman primates
that are similar to the human. Of all living animals the chimpanzee is closest to the human species, and Hamburg discusses what recent research on
chimpanzees in their natural habitat suggests about human agressiveness
and conflict resolution. It is his conclusion that aggressive behavior probably has had adaptive utility for maintaining with the environment a relationship conducive to survival and reproduction over the long course of
human development. But he emphasizes that the adaptive utility of aggressive behavior in past environments gives no assurance that similar behavior
will function adaptively in ensuring survival in the very different and

largely man-made environment of today. Hamburg points out that some of our emotional response tendencies and learning orientations are mediated by parts of the brain that are very old in the evolutionary development of man, and he speculates that these tendencies and orientations probably were built in because they worked well in adaptation over many thousands or even millions of years. Drastic changes in our physical and psychic environment have occurred since the beginning of the industrial revolution. This time interval has been too short for change to occur in the older structure of the brain, and Hamburg considers it vital to pursue research on the underlying mechanisms of neural circuitry, neural chemistry, and neural endocrinology that mediate human aggressive behavior. He also says there is great need for research directed toward more effective problem-solving processes, which will enhance the changes of making well-informed decisions in the complex, stressful situations created by today's security issues. Hamburg sees most conflicts in contemporary society arising from a pervasive human tendency to dichotomize people between a positively valued "we," or in-group, and a negatively valued "they," or out-group. He says that although the content of intergroup hostility varies widely from time to time and from place to place, the form of the antagonism is remarkably similar. Of all the technological advances of the twentieth century Hamburg considers television the most important for the future of our species because of its potential for reducing intergroup rivalry through provision of a worldwide network which can portray group diversity sympathetically while highlighting shared human experiences, even in times of stress.

Taking an overall view of the lectures, it is clear that there is more agreement than disagreement about the nature of the modern world and the critical issues of change and security confronting it. All lecturers have incorporated in their thinking, implicitly if not explicitly, a recognition that the exploitation of science and technology has changed irrevocably the conditions and the time scales that govern human affairs. With this recognition has come a realization that there is an urgent need for new ways to deal with political, economic, social, and military change, As yet, clashes between traditional ideologies and differing world views have limited the extent to which this thinking has influenced development of new ways of structuring national and international affairs. However, as is evident from these lectures, there is a growing consensus that the reality of human survival requires frontier-crossing cooperation—across intellectual and ideological as well as physical frontiers. The revolutionary events

of the past few decades have brought the world to this state. With sufficient determination the next few decades can be equally significant in
bringing about practical steps toward the new mastery man must attain
over himself and his affairs, perhaps along some of the lines suggested here.

World Change and
World Security

1

The United States and
A United Europe:
Are We Now
Uncertain Partners?

Roy Jenkins

What is a United Europe? What is the partnership it can be said to have
with the United States? Can the United States and a United Europe be
regarded as in some way comparable? What is their future? Have they one?

In dealing with these questions I intend to take up three themes: a little
history of the relationship between Americans and Western Europeans;
some description of the institutions of the European communities and
their direction of growth (this can be at best a kind of photograph taken
with a short time exposure since these institutions are evolving even as we
look at them); and some thoughts about the uncertainties latent in the relationship between the industrial societies on each side of the Atlantic.
Therein I shall try to express my own best hopes for the future.

The United States is a country in which the past has only relative virtue.
Until recently at least, the eyes of the United States have been, more perhaps than the rest of the world, focused on the future. If we are to look
forward, however, we must look backward as well. The United States is a
product of European civilization and at the same time a reaction against
European society and European politics. It was created as a revolt against
one European state, although aided in that process by another one. It was
populated to a large extent by those who for reasons of persecution or
poverty, or lack of opportunity, wished to shake the dust of Europe off
their feet. But only in a few cases was this accompanied by a desire to get
their European heritage out of their minds and hearts; rather it was to
keep Europe as a point of reference in the framework of their new society
and cherish it while adapting and, to some extent, reshaping it in their
minds.

It is not therefore surprising that one of the basic principles of U.S.
policy, at least until 1917, and to some extent well after that, was a desire
to keep free of the entanglements and sophistries of European diplomacy

and conflict. Nevertheless in this century the United States has fought two world wars, entering them both reluctantly but ineluctably, which arose— the first wholly, the second principally—from European causes. As a result of the second at least, the position of the United States in the world was dramatically changed. Then began a quarter of a century in which the United States had a pre-eminence in the world of which Washington was more assuredly the center than any capital since the fall of ancient Rome. In those postwar years the United States held the political balance of the world and on the whole welcomed the task. American withdrawal in the 1920s had gravely damaged hopes for any long-term peace. Such a withdrawal in the forties or fifties or sixties would have been infinitely more disastrous. It would have meant a fundamental shift in the balance of power toward the Soviet Union. It is no wonder that at that time the support of the United States became essential to the continued independence and prosperity of Western Europe, that most vulnerable peninsula, for such it is, at the near end of Asia.

It is likewise no surprise that the United States should have become an early, enthusiastic, and even impatient supporter of the process of European economic and political integration. Many needs and many motives pushed the United States in this direction.

There was the wholly understandable desire to avoid any repetition of what happened to this country in 1917 and 1941. Anything that the Europeans could do to put to an end forever to their civil wars, which had so devastatingly involved the world in general and the United States in particular, was obviously a prime American interest.

Americans naturally had their own inner faith in the advantages of union, of federal institutions, of what could be forged by the heat engendered by the mingling of peoples, of traditions, of customs, of ways of life. In short, many Americans saw a union of European states on the same lines as the union they had made for themselves.

There was the again the wholly understandable feeling that the Europeans should organize themselves to use as cooperatively and effectively, perhaps as economically as possible too, the massive American economic aid which was so generously and necessarily provided after the end of World War II.

There was the strong feeling, as strong today as ever, that if the United States was to accept and continue the risk of military involvement in the defense of Europe, the Europeans should organize to make the biggest and most effective contribution of their own that was possible.

From 1950 or even earlier it was therefore a settled and major object of American policy to encourage moves toward the integration of Western Europe. The recently published memoirs of Jean Monnet are studded with the names of distinguished Americans, and not only the most obvious ones, the presidents and the secretaries of state, but men such as Jack McCloy, George Ball, and Bob Bowie who were all closely and intensively involved in this most creative period of European development.

It wasn't easy in those days, and it still is not. Sometimes Americans from outside pushed harder than we did in Europe, and occasionally in directions in which the Europeans did not want to go. Thus, American desire for early German rearmament at one time endangered the setting up of the coal and steel community, and this danger was circumvented for a time only at the price of setting down what became the dead end of the European defense community. Much later in the sixties the project for a multinational nuclear force, good though its motives were, also proved an unfortunate diversion.

These exceptions illustrate the consistency and, on the whole, effectiveness of United States support for the idea of a United Europe. It is in some ways paradoxical that what was—and is—an essentially political enterprise should have been pursued by largely economic means. This was essentially because it proved easier to make the coal and steel community and, later, the European economic community than to make a European defense community or a European political community. But we should not be deceived. The European founding fathers—Robert Schuman, Conrad Adenauer, Alcide de Gasperi, Paul-Henri Spaak—were always much more interested in politics than they were in products and markets. They might have echoed the sentiments of Gladstone when fairly early in his political career he was made vice-president of the board of trade and said, "I wished to concern myself with the great affairs of men, and instead here I am set to look after packages."

But the founding fathers of Europe made a good job of looking after packages, and soon realized that the loom of trade made a tissue which included a degree of supranationality, and itself became, as it remains today, one of the great affairs of men.

At this early stage this point was perhaps better understood on this side of the Atlantic than in Europe itself. Quite often moves toward European economic integration were against the short-term trading interests of the United States, although the immense growth over the past years of the wealth and stability of the European market benefited world trade in gen-

eral and therefore the United States as a major participant in it. Happily
for us all, in those formative days there was almost invariably in Washington a willingness not only to take a long-term rather than a short-term
economic view but also to see that the political advantages of having
stable, prosperous, and united allies far outweighed any limited short-term
economic inconveniences.

Then after the early moves forward, there was the problem of Britain.
Perhaps there is always the problem of Britain. Was Europe to consist of
the Six or of a larger number? In the 1950s and 1960s the debate in Britain was about whether British relations with the countries of the continent should be more akin to those of the United States, or to their own
with each other. Was Britain's relationship with France or Germany or
Italy, Belgium or Holland or Luxemburg, to be more like that of the
United States, or was it more like that of France to Germany, or Holland
to Italy? The attitude of both the Attlee government, 1945–1951, and of
the second Churchill government which followed, thus spanning the crucial formative decade of 1945–1955, was firmly in favor of attempting for
Britain an American-style relationship with the continent of Europe, a
relationship of support from the outside, of support as Churchill once said
in defining his attitude to the Church of England, when he remarked, "I
am more a buttress of the church than the pillar: I support it from the
outside." Ernest Bevin, that most notable foreign secretary in the Attlee
government, was one of the major architects of the North Atlantic Treaty
because that was an Atlantic-style relationship; but he kept Britain firmly
out of the European steel and coal community because that was a continental relationship. Anthony Eden, foreign secretary in the second
Churchill government, tried to encourage the creation of a European defense community without Britain because we were different, although he
eventually committed British troops to Germany for the rest of the
century—which was indeed a strong commitment to enter into. He also
declined to be represented, when he had become prime minister, at the
Messina Conference in the summer of 1955 which led on directly to the
Treaty of Rome and the foundation of the European economic community. Those were the days, still more than in our days of much greater relative power in the twenties and thirties, when the British saw themselves as
the meeting point of three circles: the Commonwealth, the North Atlantic,
and Europe.

Now quite clearly in the retrospect and context of history this British
view of ourselves, however understandable at the time, held as it was by
statesmen of note and even vision, represented a gross overestimate of

British power and British options, and turned out to be a source of mis-judgment and misfortune for ourselves and our allies. It might have been expected that these illusions would have been punctured by the failure of our last imperial adventure, the Suez venture, which took place exactly twenty years ago this autumn, and to have led to the abandonment of the idea that we were a kind of mini United States off the coast of Europe. We might thus have been expected as a result of this to have been impelled toward Europe itself, and indeed in the longer term this may have been the effect. But in the shorter term the failure, the humiliating failure of Suez, affected the two countries directly concerned—France and Britain—very differently and therefore drove them apart rather than together.

The British, chastened and a little guilty, drew the conclusion that how-ever unhelpful Secretary Dulles and even President Eisenhower might have been, the main lesson to be drawn was that no more enterprises were to be attempted without the assured support of Britain's principal ally on this side of the Atlantic. Hilaire Belloc's words, "Keep-a-hold of nurse, for fear of finding something worse," became for most of the next decade Britain's firm motto for dealing with the United States. At the beginning there was even some attempt to give new life to the special relationship; but by the end nurse had become too preoccupied with her own affairs and perhaps too bespattered by the dirt of Vietnam to give even starched reassurance.

In France the reaction was quite different. There was less guilt and more anger. The lesson drawn there was not to trust the Americans and prob-ably not the British either. When General de Gaulle came to power eigh-teen months later, this turned into an intransigent but successful pursuit of French independence, with "the Anglo-Saxons" (that curious and rather mythical people) kept as far as possible at arm's length.

This conjunction of Gaullism in France and Macmillanism in Britain created delicate temptations for the United States. There was, of course, the temptation to play one off against the other. There was also the more subtle temptation to abandon faith in the idea of a united Europe and to work bilaterally through the individual European governments. On the whole these temptations were resisted. Of course some bilateralism con-tinued, as it still does, and is bound to do so as long as European institu-tions remain imperfect. But no one doubted that the Americans wanted both the enlargement and the strengthening of the European Community. Knowledge that this was so was deeply reassuring to those who like myself had the same beliefs. Even those opposed had to reckon with it. This point is well illustrated by the fact that when Hugh Gaitskell, then leader of the opposition in Britain, made what I regard as the only major political mis-judgment of his career and opposed British entry into the community in 1962, he thought it necessary to write in his own hand a thirteen page letter of justification to John Kennedy. He did what he believed to be right, as he always did, but he knew it would not be well received in Washington and thought he had better explain himself.

Those anxious and disagreeable days in this context at least are gone. The European Community now comprises both the original Six and the new Three, including Britain, who joined in 1973.

Now a word about that community and its institutions, and the way in which they are evolving. But before doing so I should like to give a warning. It is perhaps easy for Americans, particularly in their bicentennial year, to see an analogy between the United States of America and the uniting states of Europe. This is a temptation which should, I believe, be resisted, not because there is nothing in it, but because it can lead, like many historical and political analogies, to misleading hopes and expectations. In this year of 1976, Americans have probably thought more about their origins, their origin as a nation at any rate, than at any time for a century, and have better separated the fact from the fantasy of what happened two hundred years ago. As much perhaps by inadvertence as by deliberate intent, and with many deep misgivings, a group of remote colonists, as they then appeared to us, united by language, custom, and the land on which they lived, threw off the authority of a mother country which was itself divided by the constitutional issues at stake. The new country thus begun had more than a century in which to develop in relative peace, protected for the most part by the British Navy from uncomfortable involvement in the affairs of the rest of the world.

Contrast this with the origins of the European Community. The original Six had one unhappy thing in common: they had all been defeated, and in many cases devastated, in war. They had also been forcibly united for four awful years under the domination of Adolf Hitler. Their first thought was to unite to prevent at all costs a third European civil war. But as their prosperity returned—and it did after a hesitant beginning with a great surging wave which could hardly have been anticipated— as their prosperity returned they became again more conscious of their historical roots, their different languages, their different habits of thought, their different ways of life. The recovery of Europe as a whole meant a recovery in the self-confidence of the participating states. Thus what happened was in a way the reverse of what happened in America. Suppose that Massachusetts had before independence been the only British part of America, and that New Jersey had been Dutch, Rhode Island Flemish, Virginia German, Georgia

French, and Maryland Italian, and that each had proudly retained the traditions of its homeland; how difficult, of not impossible, would have been the elaboration of a federal constitution of anything like the kind that was eventually established. This persisting diversity is one of the riches of Europe; but it has required looser, different mechanisms that cannot too readily or facilely be compared with your own.

The constitution of the European communities is the Treaty of Rome in 1957 as subsequently amended. This constitution represents a balance between respect for the powers of the member states and the grant of a limited measure of supranationality in economic and judicial matters to the institutions of the communities. Four main institutions were set up, and I shall have a few words to say about each of them.

First, there is the commission of which I am president. It is the executive body of the communities and is responsible for ensuring that the principles of the treaty are observed and for initiating proposals for adoption by representatives of member states sitting together as the council. In proportion to its responsibilities the commission, often accused of vast bureaucracy, is in fact very small: some 10,000 people, of which about a third are concerned, as is inevitable, with interpretation and translation. At its head are thirteen commissioners, two each from Germany, France, Italy, and Britain, and one from each of the other five members. They are chosen by member governments, though by common accord the choice has to be endorsed by the others, and each has on assuming office to swear an oath to be guided only by the European interest rather than that of his own country. Their decisions are by majority vote.

Then there is the council, the Council of Ministers as it is normally called, the principal decision-making body responsible for coordination of the general economic policies of member states. The council consists of the representatives of each member government, and the chairmanship moves from one country to another every six months. All important decisions there, unlike in the commission, are by unanimity. The commission and the council are thereby placed in a state of what has sometimes, and perhaps appropriately, been called creative tension. At its best it is creative, at any rate.

Next there is the European Parliament, which has advisory and supervisory powers and meets eleven times a year for about a week at a time. Its committees also meet between these monthly sessions. At present it consists of members who are designated by the parliaments of member states and who are themselves members of those parliaments, but the firm intention and commitment is that elections to the parliament will be by direct universal suffrage from 1978 onward. This, which I believe will be achieved, will be a very considerable and rapid achievement. It will be only 26 years after the creation of the first community—the coal and steel community—whereas, as is sometimes forgotten, it took the United States 136 years to achieve direct election to the Senate. The parliament gives opinions on proposals of the commission, debates the activities of the community, and reviews a general report submitted annually to it by the commission. More important perhaps is its power to review the annual budget and to compel if it wishes the resignation en bloc of the thirteen members of the commission.

Finally there is the Court of Justice, composed of nine judges appointed for six-year terms by common accord of the member states. The primary function of the European court is to ensure respect for the treaty and interpret the law of the community. Its judgments are legally binding throughout member states and can override national law and bring national states to book. Not so well-known are the powers of the court to guarantee or improve the position of individuals and protect fundamental human rights.

Besides these four pillars of the European communities—the commission, the council, the parliament, and the court—has grown up another more flexible institution outside the scope of the Treaty of Rome. This is European political cooperation, and represents an attempt to coordinate the foreign policies of the Nine member states toward the outside world. This aspect of its work has no permanent staff and its secretariat simply consists of national officials who change every six months with the change in the chairmanship of the council. Thus the caravan moves from capital to capital of the community twice a year. Nevertheless this is a field in which considerable progress has recently been made. As one example, in 1975 unanimity among the Nine was achieved in over 80 percent of votes at the United Nations. You will recall that the attempt to create a European defense community failed, but that the European economic community succeeded. European political cooperation in this rather limited way in which I have described it is perhaps the embryo of the European political community without which the European union, to which member states eventually look forward, could have no meaning.

These institutions have filled their functions unevenly over the years. As a bureaucracy the commission has had its successes and has had its failures. What is not always understood is the extent to which it has been the protector of the weaker member states against the stronger ones. It is in fact the instrument of the community, the means by which its policies are put into effect, whether, for example, the common agricultural policy, the common commercial policy, or antitrust legislation. It is likewise the manager of vast funds, those required for directing the agricultural market, and the regional and social funds, both of them redistributive of wealth between the different parts of the community in intent and effect. Finally it provides an administrative framework for the coordination of the economic and monetary policies of the participating states. It will be evident that its possibilities for growth, as common action is called for in new fields, is theoretically limitless, but it is at once the creature of the treaty and the servant of the council. Needless to say it comes into conflict from time to time with the member governments which, like all governments, are jealous of their powers.

Hence the importance of the Council of Ministers where the commission proposes but the council disposes. The council meets at the level of ministers of foreign affairs, but there are specialist councils as well, where such ministers as those of agriculture, finance or environment can come together.

More recently summit meetings of heads of government of the community have taken place on a regular basis three times a year and are known, somewhat confusingly, as European councils. The advantages of such meetings are obvious, but the disadvantages are less so because European councils, meetings of heads of government, provide an all-too-convenient means for ministers of foreign affairs not to take the decisions themselves but to refer them to their heads of government; and so far the heads of government meetings have often been too informal, perhaps too short, to produce the real results now required of them. Whether for this reason or for others the normal councils have in the last few years lost some of the impetus, the accommodating spirit, the readiness to take decisions which characterized the councils of the first few years in the life of the community. The requirement of unanimity of all matters of importance has laid an inevitably deadening hand.

If the commission has sometimes been too bureaucratic and the council too mindful of national interests, the parliament, through no fault of its own, has not yet succeeded in achieving adequate power of democratic control. I believe that the recent agreement on direct elections by universal suffrage will eventually give the parliament a new and different role, although direct elections will not mean any formal increase in powers. Parliaments have always traditionally been keenly interested in the problems of financial supply and control of the budget. The role of the European Parliament in helping us to tackle the problems that now face the commu-

nity—from the size and purposes of the budget to the lack of economic
balance between the member states—may well prove to be crucial. But
again it will not be easy. National parliaments are in no hurry to give up
their powers; and a whole new balance of democratic power within the
community will eventually have to be established.

Finally in this section, a word on the European court. Here there are
remarkable possibilities for growth. The powers of the court are more formidable because it is in effect, although international, a judicial organ of
each member state and its decisions are directly enforceable. The implications go very far indeed for those used to the doctrine of absolute parlia-
mentary sovereignity—which is particularly so in Britain, where the
somewhat extreme position of Dicey has long held sway. To take one example, an individual could invoke the decisions of the court on equal pay
for equal work if he found that British or Italian or German legislation on
these points did not go as far as the Treaty of Rome. I think that even
Americans, used to the Supreme Court, would be startled by the potential
powers of the European court. The best American analogy I can think of
would be to have the Equal Rights Amendment automatically becoming
part of the law of the United States not because it had been passed by
Congress but by virtue of a judgment of the International Court of Justice
at the Hague. In due course in my view the European court may play as
formative a part in the history of Europe as Marshall's Supreme Court
played in the early to middle history of the United States.

It will be clear from all I have said that although the European Community in its various aspects has economic, political, and judicial reality, it is
very far from complete. Moreover the relationship between the community and the member states is constantly shifting. It would also, I am
afraid, be a mistake to think that the construction of the community while
it may be slow is always advancing. In fact I do not think that any part
that has been built has yet been demolished, or that work in this area, or
that has ever been more than blocked. But the community has faced, and
now faces, very serious problems.

I shall mention only one of them: the economic capacities of the member states, far from reaching a rough equivalence, have recently become
more markedly divergent than ever before. Four years ago, before that
perhaps, the small countries feared the dominance of the four large ones:
France, Germany, Britain, and Italy. Two years ago there was fear of the
two most successful large countries: Germany and France. Now Germany
is alone in a position different from the others. A number of ideas are

under discussion for righting a disequilibrium which no one wants, least of all the Germans. But these ideas would if applied require discipline and sacrifice on the part of those who have dropped behind. I do not know which will be adopted. But I do know that if this fundamental problem is not faced the effect will be that of an earth tremor on a half-built house.

It would be tempting for the United States to think it better to leave the Europeans to put their affairs in order and develop the new institutions I have described, and deal for the time being with the familiar governments of the member states. It is not necessarily easy to conduct business with an institution which so evidently has scaffolding still around it, where fierce argument comes from within, where parts seem half built and others half used, where the telephone system does not seem to be fully installed, and where sometimes even essential services do not seem to be laid on. Yet this would be a great mistake. At least most of the building is in good working order and is stronger than it sometimes looks. And the view from the top, to which men of vision occasionally still mount, reveals far horizons.

I do not want to numb you with figures but one or two statistics about the community and the states which comprise it will give you an idea of its scope and potentialities. In 1975 the total population was just short of 260 million, against 212 million for the United States and 110 million for Japan. Its gross domestic product was $1,362 billion against $1,505 billion for the United States and $491 billion for Japan. The volume of its imports (*excluding* trade among its members) was $155 billion against $97 billion for the United States and $58 billion for Japan; and the volume of its exports (again *excluding* trade among member states) was $150 billion against $108 billion for the United States and $56 billion for Japan. Thus you will see that the European Community comprises an immense population, a gross domestic product almost but not quite as big as that of the United States, and a volume of imports and exports that make it decisively the largest trading unit in the world.

No wonder that President Carter wrote:

United States-European relations is at the heart of U.S. foreign policy. In economic policy, their cooperation with each other and with Japan is necessary both to their prosperity and to the progress of developing countries; growing European units can help to fulfill this promise.

He later added:

Europe will be better able to fulfill its role in U.S.-European-Japanese cooperation in the degree that it can speak with one voice and act with one will. The United States has sometimes seemed to encourage European unification with words, while preferring to deal with national governments in practice. I believe that we should deal with Brussels on economic issues to the extent that the Europeans themselves make Brussels the focus of their decisions.

I much welcome these words of President Carter. They represent a challenge to the institutions of the community and the member states to rise above their various national problems and difficulties, and to negotiate with the strength only unity can give them. The European Community is more than the sum of its parts; and it is generous as well as sensible of the United States president to have given the Europeans the encouragement he now has.

I say sensible as well as generous because the community, with all its imperfections, is gradually asserting greater weight and authority in the world. In Europe itself the community has acted as a political as well as an economic magnet. The Six original members were joined by the Three nearly four years ago. Around this central nucleus is a web of association agreements with all the free countries of Europe. Greece is now negotiating for membership, and Portugal is not far behind. Spain may follow, and also Turkey. The community has also drawn closer to such countries as Yugoslavia and those of the southern and eastern shores of the Mediterranean, and through its mechanisms of political cooperation is engaged in a dialogue with the Arab world, where it has still greater economic interests than has the United States. It is in the process of working out new economic relations with the countries of Eastern Europe and the Soviet Union, and of course played a major role in the Conference on Security and Cooperation in Europe, which led to that charter of hope for all Europeans on either side of the postwar dividing line: the Helsinki Declaration.

Looking beyond the frontiers of Europe, we can see the network of agreements with the 49 African, Caribbean, and other countries comprised in the Lomé Convention. The community thus has an intimate institutional relationship with a large number of countries in the Third World, and is the source of both more trade and more aid than the United States itself. Looking still further afield, the community has a particular relationship with the Chinese People's Republic, which was the first communist country to accredit an ambassador to the community in Brussels.

I need hardly say that the very success of the community and its members in the fields I have described is of vital concern to the United States. It means that the Europeans have been taking on an increasingly important part of the burden of responsibility for the maintenance and development of the democratic industrial society we have in common. It means that in the eyes of the Third World there is more than one source of Western power, and that on the international as on the national scale we practice what we preach about plurality of choice. I would not deny that in another sense the growing trading weight of the European community can complicate life for the United States by adding a new dimension of difficulty and argument, and by bringing new and sometimes divergent interests into play. But I have no doubt that when these considerations are weighed against each other the balance is overwhelmingly positive for the United States. The world can now be a less lonely place for a country with the power and responsibilities of America.

I have not so far spoken about problems of defense. Like the Pope, the commission has no divisions. Nevertheless the defense of Europe cannot be dissociated from the recovery of Europe and the growth of the new European institutions. I have already referred to the failure of the proposal for a European defense community in the 1950s; and there would of course be many practical objections to reviving such an idea now. The fundamental point perhaps is that the proper unit of defense is not Western Europe or the Europe of the community but the North Atlantic area as a whole. Western defense is at present organized in a way which respects the specifically European as well as the broadly Atlantic aspect. Thus there is our joint membership of the North Atlantic Treaty, a more restricted membership of that strictly practical European defense association called the Euro-Group, and the still more restricted membership of the Western European Union which involves its seven signatories in the most binding commitment into which any state can enter: an automatic commitment to mutual defense. It is much tighter than the North Atlantic Treaty. If these perspectives are to change, and change they may like all perspectives in the years to come, I think that the main agent of such change will be the need for the Europeans to integrate their own defense industries, to standardize equipment among themselves and within the alliance, and to establish a more even partnership, each making its due contribution, with the United States.

The more powerful the European Community becomes, the greater its capacity to be a worthy partner of the United States. This is as true in the realm of defense as it is in any other. The converse is equally true. If the community were to fall apart and the national states were to try to go their separate ways, the capacity of the Europeans to contribute to the common defense and play the greater role which should surely come to them over the years would be gravely prejudiced. NATO came before the community, but I doubt very much whether it could now survive the disintegration of the community. And the community's relationship with countries at present outside its bounds—with Greece, with Turkey, with Spain, with Portugal in particular—can have considerable impact on the political orientation of those countries.

So far the partnership across the Atlantic has been unequal. In many respects it remains so. To that extent it remains an uncertain partnership, one with immense possibilities for the future but one which could still go wrong.

I deal here first with the economic aspects. Here there is in fact a very lopsided balance of trade in favor of the United States. This is not perhaps surprising. Unlike the community the United States is self-sufficient in most raw materials and does much less trade with the outside world. The American consumer tends to buy American more than the European consumer buys European. And foreign competition is more deeply embedded in our home market than it is in yours. Moreover we manage our agricultural market in a different way, and in certain cases give preference to agricultural products from the countries with which the community has institutional links or which come under the Generalized Preference Scheme.

Nevertheless the United States has an enormous trade surplus with the community (in 1975 it was over $6 billion and in 1976 will probably run to over $7 billion). Even in the field of agriculture alone the United States had a surplus of $4.5 billion in 1975. This is hardly a picture of a trading relationship with a protectionist Europe. There has been, is, and, I imagine, is always likely to be, some commercial friction between such giant economic entities as the United States and the community; but I hope some of the issues over which our negotiators contend will find their solution in the multilateral trade negotiations which we would like to see completed by the end of next year. Certainly if we ever got near to a trade war with each other there could be only one certain result: grave damage to us both and, in the present fragile state of world trade, grave damage to the world as a whole. Let us have greater mutual understanding. Trading means buying as well as selling, and in a political as well as an economic perspective a grossly unequal balance of trade is not in the long run tolerable to either partner across the Atlantic.

It is sometimes said that the European Community is an economic giant but a political dwarf. This is half-true, but only to the extent that we Europeans make it so. The United States today, I suspect, does not see a political community in Europe in the way that it sees and deals with an economic community. This is illustrated I think by the fact that the limited and strictly economic and unimaginative term of the Common

Market is almost invariably used in this country. You may notice that I
have not used it once this evening. That is at once natural and purposeful
for me. There is of course a common market in Europe. But there is an
attempt at, and half a reality of, something much deeper, and that mixture
of reality and aspiration is far better expressed by the term European
Community. I hope that phrase will pass into wider use in this country, for
phrases have a power that is more than purely descriptive. And it would be
ironical and perverse if leaders of United States opinion, which for a generation have been attracted by the political unity of Europe, were now to
discount that aspect of the enterprise. So long as the economic community is a flourishing concern, there is a certain logic driving its members
towards at least political cooperation and perhaps one day a full political
community; but if the economic community looks sick and the economics
of its member states diverge, so the machinery of political cooperation
looks sick too, and cooperation, let alone anything more ambitious, becomes increasingly hard to attain.

In this respect I would like to make a simple plea to Europeans and
Americans alike. It is that President Carter's words to the effect that
Europe would be better able to fulfill its role if it could speak with one
voice and act with one will should be heeded by all. I include Americans
in my plea because if the United States searches for one European voice
and one European will, it will be more likely to find them that if it pre-
fers to look for nine European voices and nine European wills.

The words of the Gettysburg address are, I suppose, almost the most
overworked in the American branch of the English language. They could
not possibly be quoted straight. But I am occasionally tempted to para-
phrase them into a modern European context.

Two decades and a few years ago our fathers brought forth upon this
European continent a new Community, conceived in hope and dedicated
to the proposition that all European nations depend for their strength,
security, and prosperity upon each other. Now we are engaged in a great
trial of will, testing whether that Community or any Community so conceived, can long endure.

We do not, of course, have the challenge of a European civil war. Such
wars are, I hope, behind us. But we do have the threats of inertia, or paro-
chialism, of narrow nationalism, and, through misplaced and unimaginative caution, of standing still when immobility is a much greater risk than
moving forward. I think we can overcome these dangers. If I thought
otherwise, I would not have taken this assignment. But it will be a struggle.
Walt Whitman, I think, wrote nearer to the Charles River than Abraham
Lincoln spoke. "Have the elder races faltered, Do they droop and end their

lesson Over there beyond the seas?" he asked about 100 years ago.

My answer today is "No." We are engaged in an enterprise even more difficult and complicated than your own two hundred years ago. We need understanding perhaps more than help, patience more than pressure to act in ways that may not be our own. The result can be of vast benefit, not only to us but to you. The more equal the partnership between the United States and the *uniting* states of Europe the better for both, and the longer it will endure.

2

Security in a Changing World

Willy Brandt

"World Change and World Security"—the title of this lecture series—is factual, it sounds almost dry and scientific. The circumstances to which it points are dramatic.

The change our world is undergoing is no longer limited in scope or going at an easy pace. We live in a period in which radical scientific, political, and social changes quickly penetrate peoples' minds.

The age of upheaval began many years ago. Most of us in the industrial nations in West and East hardly took any notice at the beginning; we concerned ourselves with other things, we flew to the moon, we entrenched ourselves behind sophisticated armaments. The globe, in the grip of the two superpowers, seemed to be divided and fairly consolidated. Very few were aware of how very fragile and misleading it was. There were not many people who realized early enough how much the industrial societies would be pressed by new problems and what was emerging, especially in those parts of the world not enjoying the privilege of belonging to the club of industrialized nations. Hardly anyone among the leading statesmen of the world had the strength or the vision to prepare his country and all of us in time for development in those countries we have come to call the Third World.

By now many have understood that world security is not simply a question of military balance; in addition, and even more clearly, it is a question of how causes of conflicts can be eliminated by economic equilibrium and the organization of peaceful cooperation. There is no longer only a first, second, third, or fourth world; there is the same *one* world, to go back to Wendell Wilkie, one world in which nations have to remember their mutual dependence, or else they will survive this age not at all or only after disasters.

I am not speaking of apocalyptic last days' visions, nor of the imminent end of the world. We know that such tendencies enter the discussion time and again in certain intervals. Mostly they are not beneficial warnings, but signs of a crisis consciousness with which one had not come to terms. I saw in my part of the world that this was the soil on which the weeds of totalitarianism flourished.

It is thus not my intention to generate a mood of crisis. I want to discuss what we need; an awareness of our situation; a sense of the reality in which we live today; intensive work to find the answers to the not-so-new questions pressing us.

How is it that these not-so-new urgent questions were repressed for so long? I think because the political systems of the Western democracies are not geared for early diagnosis. In their present constitution they are comparatively efficient repair institutions. But their present constitution (in the sense of condition) is not God-given. We must therefore improve our political systems—which is a great task. It includes among other things capacities for long-range analysis, greater demands on published opinion, political groupings guided by ideas and not only fixated to competition for power.

In this context I start from one premise: We do not live in a short-term exceptional situation which later on may swing back to the normal situation of the allegedly "good old times." It can be predicted that for all foreseeable time mankind will be faced with more problems than can be solved quickly enough. The realistic objective must be to keep this dangerous disparity within the narrowest limits.

Drastic changes in all states of the world—industrial states, rising, raw materials-possessing countries of the Third World, or the very poor (least developed) countries—will not be without repercussions on the network of international relations linking all of them together.

The network, to continue this metaphor, at present shows dangerous strains in more than one place. Countries where development advances too slowly or hardly at all can no longer put up with the fact that the disparity between them and the rich nations of the Northern hemisphere continues to grow—and this should not surprise anybody! They demand new, more just principles of order for the world economy. Our countries will not be allowed to evade this, even if they cannot bring themselves to like some of the proposed models. Justice demands—and if we do not want to listen to justice, reason will tell us—that there never will be a lasting and secure coexistence of affluence and misery.

The relatively rich nations will have to make up their minds in good time
to make material concessions. History demonstrates, I think, that it never
made sense to try and hold overdue bastions with a last great summoning
of strength.

Why should we want to play the role of unyielding bosses of past generations once again? At that time, too, and in some places even today, there
have been attempts to deny the rising working class its rights. To no avail.
On the contrary, it can be said: Without the increase in mass incomes and
the progress made in social policy, capitalism presumably would not have
remained viable.

In the relationship between North and South we shall perhaps be able to
prevent overreactions by joint intelligent action: The discrimination of the
have-nots is not to be replaced by the denouncement of the haves. When
we speak of justice in the context of the world economy, this means on
the one hand that the transfer of resources to the Third World must be
increased and brought into some systematic order. But it means also that
patent solutions that would endanger the economic cycle in the industrialized world are of no use to anybody. We need reason on all sides.

Let me add at this point that the industrial states under Communist rule,
too, bear responsibility for what happens in the world. They cannot free
themselves from it in the long run. We must point out to them that they
would be well-advised to prepare themselves for international discussions
and negotiations on raw materials, trade, and development aid.

You will perhaps remember that in Boston the president of the World
Bank suggested that aspects of the North-South issue be examined by an
independent commission. My name was mentioned in this context and I
have had a number of discussions with Mr. McNamara about this. Regardless of how much time I shall be able to devote to it until the end of 1978,
I want to say here and now that the proposed independent commission
will not be able to relieve the governments of any of the problems that are
being negotiated at present. The North-South dialogue in particular has to
make progress if more far-reaching considerations are not to remain pending. Besides, it cannot be a matter of "mediation," as one reads in the
press here and there, but rather of working out essentials for the eighties,
following the tradition of what was written down for the seventies under
the responsibility of our Canadian colleague, Lester Pearson.

The smouldering North-South conflict is certainly not the only world
economic source of danger from which world political calamity may arise.

High balance of payment deficits and an international monetary system
that has become out of order inflation and unemployment, shortage of
energy, and costly strains on the environment—these and others are characteristics of our difficult reality. A thinker of the standing of Carl Friedrich
von Weizsacker, the German philosopher, believes it an open question as to
how far the superpowers could keep up their intention to prevent war
when faced with the political unrest that would be linked—inevitably, as
he wrote in his last book—with long-term stagnation or shrinking of the
world market.

At any rate, we see every day how many of the international and
internal economic problems derive from the disorder of the world
economy. We have a direct and far-reaching national and international
interest in our governments coming together to make important joint
efforts, and must insist on it. None of the great problems facing us today
will improve by being shelved. What we need is conscious, purposeful,
future-oriented action.

I think, therefore, that the governments of the leading nations in world
trade should envisage adequate international demand especially for capital
goods in order to bring about a general rise in employment. Unemployment will not disappear if we rely only on the much invoked self-healing
forces. World trade may be threatened again if we have to allow the return
of laboriously reduced trade barriers. Energy policy—including a more
intelligent management of resources—greatly requires national planning
and international cooperation.

Changed economic conditions strongly suggest that we change our attitude in many respects. When growth is no longer a matter of course or
quasi-automatic and has therefore less priority, there is need for more
imagination and more conscious, coordinated action.

In my view this is one of the great challenges: to further develop the
democratic order in such a way that it neither leaves the field to rival
groups nor makes way for the rule of freedom-stifling bureaucracies,
governmental or nongovernmental.

I believe that we are forced to review, within our societies as well as in
the relationship between nations, claims that have arisen from the idea of
automatic growth. Individual interests must be integrated more firmly into
an overall social solidarity. There must be greater awareness of the fact
that the freedom of the individual and freedom of all depend on each
other. Above all, the impression must not prevail that the problems of the
future can not be coped with, the impression that the forces of progress
have given up. The order of freedom will continue to exist only if we

succeed in establishing new confidence in and through this order. Great demands will be made on the capability of innovation, on our moral strength, and on the consciousness of man. In everyday political life there must result, I am convinced, in the realization that important government decisions are to be taken in close coordination with the citizens concerned or interested. In economic and social policy there is the need for the closest possible cooperation between the state, the employers, and the trade unions. I do not want to propagate German models, but along the lines of what we call codetermination there is the chance of equilibrium and overall responsibility.

The tasks are too great to be solved by one individual nation; in saying this I do not exclude America. We stand a good chance only if we extend our knowledge and our capacities by even closer international cooperation. It is not sufficient to discuss whether it would be politically desirable to reduce to a reasonable level the thinking in terms of national sovereignty and to develop new forms of frontier-crossing cooperation: the pressure of circumstances, correctly understood, leaves us no other choice.

The subject of this lecture series puts to us the question of how we can maintain or achieve security in a changing world. International politics must, to an increasing extent, be general staff work for peace. The roads we have to walk for peace will be dangerous roads for a long time to come. We must not shirk them if we want to safeguard more security in the world.

I shall now speak of the relationship, somewhat changed but still not undangerous, between West and East. The United States in the years past made great efforts to ease relationships with the Soviet Union and with the People's Republic of China. Suspicion arose occasionally in Europe that the great powers might come to an understanding over the heads of their respective allies. I have never agreed with this but tried to see to it that my country made its own appropriate contribution; our treaties with our Eastern neighbors had—and still have—their specific significance.

I want to encourage explicitly responsible leaders in your country to do everything within their power to bring about for all of us, within the alliance and beyond, a higher degree of security. In this sense I should consider it important and useful if a SALT II agreement, an agreement on the second phase of controlling nuclear arms between the United States and the Soviet Union, could be negotiated.

Whoever takes an unbiased look at the situation in Europe and compares it to the conditions of fifteen or twenty years ago will see that peace in our part of the world is today a little bit less endangered. There is no reason for exaggeration. And yet because of Berlin the Third World War had been in the air, comparable to the crisis in Cuba. And there was more than one occasion when one could tremble for the fate of Western Europe.

With our efforts for détente—and I hope I understand it correctly, détente is not a dirty word anymore—with our efforts for détente we did not eliminate the differences in systems and ideologies. But at least we have filled up some of the trenches the Cold War created in the course of many years. Economic and scientific cooperation between East and West could be increased for the benefit of both sides. Cultural exchange has improved, even though many wishes remained unfulfilled. In some areas, in particular between the two parts of Germany, some relief for the people was achieved; however, the borders remain much more closed than is desirable. Of course we must be aware of this, and we must be aware of the fact that progress in the humanitarian field too is always dependent on how the governments concerned interpret their own interests.

The Helsinki Conference in the summer of 1975 marked a step forward. I know that in the U.S.A. there is, or there has been, a tendency to take a skeptical view of that conference. Therefore I would like to emphasize that, in spite of all the differences that cannot be negotiated away, important declarations of intent and guidelines for relations were agreed upon in Helsinki. All European states except Albania accepted this. And we should not forget that the United States and Canada were participants in the conference and signed its documents. What does this mean? It means that in addition to the rights resulting from the Second World War, the corresponsibility of Americans for the political destiny of Europe can now also be based on Helsinki; it has gained a new quality, an additional quality. It is my impression that up to now this has not been adequately understood by large parts of the American public.

That conference at Helsinki was an important event, even though in retrospect the question arises of whether it has been wise to have the subject matter dealt with in a bureaucratic rather than a political manner over a period of three years. The demand for detailed conference texts did also contribute to the fact that hopes were aroused in many people in East and West, hopes that for the time being cannot be met by the European reality. The contrast between fundamentally different political systems just cannot be resolved by compromise formulas or conjurations. Communism will not be talked away, nor will it be abolished by the drafting of texts! But it is worthwhile to negotiate on concrete questions and to fight for beliefs.

I believe that there is no reasonable alternative for the policy of détente. It must continue to be a policy that is strong in itself; only a policy aiming at a secure peace for all deserves to be called a policy of strength. This implies that concepts are developed in time to prevent a standstill. I am afraid that the Western world has not made sufficient intellectual effort to develop a policy for the time after Helsinki.

This year officials of the governments involved are to meet in Belgrade to start examining what has become of the decisions of the summer of 1975. There, in my opinion, one should not hold a tribunal but draw a factual balance, and above all one should not forget to agree on further steps forward on the basis of Helsinki.

Our interest should be concentrated on the question of what can be brought forward in conformity with the declaration jointly adopted in Helsinki. Nothing will be achieved by illusions. I think it would be advisable on the one hand not to place too high expectations on the Belgrade meeting. On the other hand, political leaders on both sides—and on the side of the nonaligned—would be well-advised if as a result of Helsinki they could concentrate on a few concrete tasks in the coming years. It would be useful to combine this with a realistic stocktaking that does not conceal disappointments.

The texts of Helsinki have been published in the press of the Eastern European states. On the basis of these texts—and the constitutions of the countries concerned—a moving struggle on human and civil rights has arisen in some places; the Prague "Charter 77" is an eloquent sign of this. Nobody can be indifferent to this development. However, nobody will be helped by our making promises we cannot keep.

I agree with President Carter when he makes it clear that our concern for human rights is indivisible. Freedom from fear and freedom from misery will for a long time to come impose obligations on us and on those who will come after us—regardless of where they live. I do not see any contradiction between our defense of human rights and the pursuit of détente. Détente is a matter of making peace in general more secure, however much the political orders are opposed to one another, and of letting factual cooperation develop where a common denominator can be found for the interests of states under very different rules; this will also mean concrete help for the individual.

Making peace more secure implies further arrangements in the military sector. If negotiations on the SALT II agreement were to be completed soon, an important prerequisite would be fulfilled for making progress in the negotiations on a mutual and balanced reduction of forces and armaments in Europe, negotiations that have been going on in Vienna for some years.

The aim of détente policy in this field must be to bring about, step by step, a situation in which a military attack without prior buildup will be impossible or almost impossible. In this connection the problem of the warning time has its specific importance.

What I have in mind is that the states involved, the countries involved, should bring themselves at least not to increase the forces now present in central Europe as long as the MBFR—Mutual Balanced Force Reductions—negotiations are pending and to conclude the so-called definition phase soon. Without losing sight of the objective of a genuine balance (the so-called parity), two further steps could then be considered: a first, though hardly more than symbolic, reduction of Soviet and American forces within the geographical limits defined in Vienna; and subsequently a first, though understandably modest, limitation of other forces within the same limits.

Such steps could be an indication of whether the negotiating parties are serious about MBFR, and they could be the starting point for further important measures to build up confidence.

Nobody will be surprised that the state of crisis of the world economy does not particularly favor the economic unification of Western Europe. Ambitious projects that were planned in the past few years had to be postponed. Instead, one concentrated on securing what had been achieved and on making the best use of the well-established possibilities of cooperation.

What we have is already more than a union for economic purposes only. The European Community advances slowly enough, yet it is becoming a political factor of some weight. Nevertheless, it will take much longer than the optimistic federalists believed before the European nations with their old independent traditions will have grown together into a new unity.

An important decision is now pending. National parliaments in the countries of the European Community will have to decide in the coming months whether the first direct elections for the European Parliament will be held next year. The result and the timetable for the decisions are not yet certain. I do hope that the objections will be overcome, but I would not be surprised if new delays arose. If the decision came about, we would have gained quite something. Europe would have given a signal that it wants to continue to work for the goal of unification also under adverse conditions. A new experience would then be to see how a parliament will develop whose powers would be very limited at the beginning.

At any rate it is certain that an internationally strengthened community will be in a better position to meet its share of responsibility in world politics, as a force of equilibrium and moderation, and also as a future-oriented example for all those who want to take a new course.

In this context it can be said with justification that the cause of democracy—contrary to the prediction of the pessimists—is not in retreat in our part of the world. As you know, the past two years have seen great changes in Southern Europe.

Almost three years ago Portugal ventured to break away from dictatorship to democracy. Not much imagination was needed to foresee that this would be a very difficult way. Many who could have helped preferred to wait and see; in America too the situation was at first not judged correctly. I say this without exaggeration: that the fascist regime was not followed by a Communist one in 1975 had something to do with the fact that some of us did not leave our friends in Portugal alone.

In Greece, the dictatorship was defeated almost at the same time. That country too needs the active solidarity of its European friends. Let me add that it also needs an image of America that is different from the one conveyed by the suspected support of the junta.

Spain, which makes important efforts—with great maturity—to heal the wounds of the past and to catch up with the democracies of Western Europe by a peaceful restructuring of its society, also needs understanding and the preparedness for cooperation. It can help to provide Europe with new strength.

Italy for many reasons found it more difficult than its northern neighbors to adjust its economy and to reach an internal balance. We would be ill-advised, I think, if we were to neglect this country or discourage its democratic forces.

In France, political weights have definitely shifted during the past few years. There can be no question of an imminent seizure of power by the Communists. The Democratic Socialists have again become a strong party. In the eyes of many French citizens they prove to be a force which would be able to assume national responsibility.

I want to leave it at these few remarks. In America one need not be overly concerned about Western Europe. The slowly uniting Europe will be pluralistic; the forces of social democracy, of democratic socialism, will have considerable weight in this Europe—I think not to its disadvantage. But these forces of the European Left have more in common with the great liberal tradition of America than many people realize.

The relationship between North America and Europe continues to be an important, constant factor in the work for peace in the world. America is, similar to the Soviet Union, though more indirectly, also a European power. And Europe continues to be one of the factors that determines America's security and well-being.

The cooperation between the United States of America and the uniting states of Europe in principle requires no change. It is close and trustful. It is well-established and will always be able to overcome occasional differences of opinion.

In this context we hardly need any new concepts, but what we need is an ever-renewed preparedness to stand up for each other and to tackle joint tasks. Economic development especially has made it clear to us that none of us can cope with our problems without the cooperation of our partners.

As far as the military field is concerned, it is clear to me that for us in Europe there will be no security without the protection and the guarantee by the United States, but that on the other hand the United States would get into a most precarious situation if—starting from Europe—the balance of power changed significantly.

The partnership across the Atlantic thus is indispensable. It need not be re-established, but we can expand it and supplement it beyond the existing close cooperation among the governments, military staffs, and multi-national companies. Much can still be done to foster and improve the mutual understanding of the peoples. We can share more of our experiences. We should encourage direct communication between citizens as they are represented in economic organizations and trade unions, in political parties and associations, intensify contacts between universities, church, and private organizations.

I am well aware that you in the United States and we in Europe look back to some very different experiences and traditions. I know that this results here and there in very marked differences, which make it difficult to live together. And yet most of the problems facing us today are not fundamentally different, in the United States or in Europe. The question of what are the working conditions of industrial or office workers arises both here and there. Both of us must be concerned about the question of which educational system is best suited to promote the individual and to serve at the same time the objective of full employment. The threat to the environment and the need for new communications systems, energy supply, and town planning are urgent problems on both sides of the Atlantic.

Europe must, and wants, to see itself as a factor of peace. Security is its foundation, military leverage is not its first priority. Europe will wish to contribute its economic and intellectual resources in order that the urgent problems of mankind can be solved in world-wide cooperation.

Work for this objective will never end. Mankind will always be faced with new problems. And the world will always have a desire for security. In our endeavors we reckon with both these realities, and if we do so we stand a chance of organizing peace in such a way that it can be lasting and secure.

3

The Americans
and the U.S.S.R.

McGeorge Bundy

The problem of how to think about relations between the United States and the Soviet Union has, of course, been a persistent one over the last two generations. The way we ought to think about it comes up from time to time in a rather lively manner in the way our headlines run and the way our own national arguments go. One need not labor the importance of the subject. We know and they know that these are the two societies with the most obvious capacity to make the future unendurable for each other and for many others. We are thus necessarily concerned with, engaged by, occasionally preoccupied by, one another. The difficulty of the subject is also clear, certainly in this city. We know that both the political and the technical analysis have become less and less simple as we have learned more about each other. In the face of this importance and this difficulty, what I would like to think about with you is the question of how the United States gets it head together on this general topic, and what stirs me is a very interesting collection of recent events here in our own political scene.

The first set of impressions, which I at least have had, coming out of the period of the transition from one administration to another, was that, contrary to the widespread impression that many have shared in the years that followed Vietnam and Watergate, there would in fact be for the new administration a relatively wide latitude in decision and action on the international scene. One could begin with the fairly obvious fact that the national election was not decided on international grounds. One could continue with the evident revival of a relatively balanced belief that the United States did in fact have inescapable responsibilities and opportunities. One could go on with the apparent ability of the president to staff his administration in a manner that seemed satisfactory to him. And one could add that there seemed no reason why he should not make his own choice, within a wide national consensus, as to the course that he would take in such matters as disarmament negotiation or human rights or the national defense posture of the United States.

There have been elections that did turn on foreign issues and on a sharply perceived difference between candidates. There was one in 1964 (however ironic some of the results may have been), in which Senator Goldwater clearly was rejected in part because he was thought to be outside the national consensus in his attitudes toward international affairs, and conspicuously toward the Soviet Union. There was another in 1972 when Senator McGovern, whatever his other qualities, fell out of the national consensus on the other side. But 1976 was not such an election. And so it appears that there was, as I suggest, a new freedom of executive opportunity and perhaps a new hope that an executive would act under conditions and in a manner that would be different from the personalism and secretiveness that characterized the preceding decade. The president would have room to move.

The second set of events raised a rather interesting question about that hypothesis, first in the nomination of Theodore Sorensen to the directorship of the Central Intelligence Agency and then, perhaps more seriously (because the mere personal and even accidental objections were not so great), in the nomination of Paul Warnke to be negotiator on disarmament and director of the Arms Control and Disarmament Agency. In the Warnke case there developed in the Senate a sharp division, a division exemplified in the final vote of 58 to 40 on that part of Mr. Warnke's assignment relating to negotiation. Fifty-eight votes is less than the two-thirds that will be needed if and when there is a treaty to which the senate may be asked to give its consent.

So the question I found myself asking myself was, Which is it? Is there a new freedom for the president to lead in this area or is there a brutal division within the country which sharply constrains what our government can do? And how does this affect not only what is going on but what should be going on? It is not clear a priori, especially in the light of the events of the last decade, that the presidency is always right or that the presidency should always be unfettered and, on the other hand, no one who lives in the American constitutional tradition can suppose that debate is in and of itself wicked.

In thinking about this question, I was led to ask myself about the way it has been in the period since we began to have an operational relationship with the Soviet Union. The problem of what Americans think about Communist Russia has been a serious one, of course, since 1917, but I would argue that in terms of the large-scale behavior of nations and the working responsibilities of this country that question does not become a big one until after the fall of France in 1940. Moreover, setting that year as a starting point has the advantage that I can remember it, and I do believe that is an advantage when trying to think about the way Americans think, because although one is always in danger of saying that Americans in a given year were thinking what I was thinking or what my friends were thinking, nonetheless, even if you are unrepresentative and your opinion was not majority opinion, there is advantage in having lived in the atmosphere of the arguments of a given period.

In any event, let me take you briefly through some of the extraordinary things that have happened since we found ourselves locked on the world stage with no exit that would not lead to disaster, on a stage which also included as a major player the Soviet Union. That has not been a simple relationship at any time on either side, and the best students are those who have known and shown that. Yet simplifying for argument and focusing on the question of how Americans have thought about it, I think it can be said that on our side, through most of that period, there have been two starting points, one of hope and one of fear, sometimes one of hope inspired by fear. There have been both optimism and pessimism about prospective Soviet behavior, both generous and harsh judgments about past Soviet behavior. It has gone on a long time now and has engaged a lot of people: eight presidents from Franklin Delano Roosevelt to Jimmy Carter, eleven secretaries of state from Cordell Hull to Cyrus Vance. And only in one relatively brief period in that time has there been a predominantly single-minded approach on the American side, and that is the period which coincides pretty closely with the last years of Stalin's regime and the beginnings of the thaw after his death, a period running roughly from 1947, the announcement of the Truman Doctrine, to 1955, a year of very intense Soviet-American negotiation, the year in which, for example, the Austrian State Treaty was concluded. You can argue that the period of unilateral or monolithic tension continued until John Foster Dulles' illness, but I would be inclined to a different view on that question and say that from 1955, and still more after his second election, President Eisenhower began to concern himself with both hope and fear in his thinking about the Soviet Union.

Even in that single-minded period from the Truman Doctrine through the ascendancy of Foster Dulles, the mood of the country in this context was primarily defensive. It was the estimate of the Soviet threat, not so much to us as to friends in Western Europe, that was controlling in the formation of the policy in which Dean Acheson had so important a role; and it was the view that godless Communism was the major international menace that moved Mr. Dulles and, to a lesser degree, his president in the early years of the Eisenhower Administration. Looking back, one may find it easy to conclude that this was a part of a concerted effort toward some kind of American hegemony. It is important, I think, to remember that in the context of what was actually happening, as the Soviet Union tightened its grip on Eastern Europe and conspicuously on Czechoslovakia in those years, in the context also of deeply felt weakness in the war-torn nations of Western Europe, what was felt was that this effort was a defense of freedom.

But I don't need to press that argument here because it is not my main point. My point is rather that through most of the period after 1940, going back to Franklin Roosevelt and the war and carrying through in later administrations, the approaches of the government and the desires of the public were dual, not monolithic. At most stages there was an effort at agreement as well as an effort to sustain effective containment of those Soviet pressures that were felt to be illegitimate or dangerous, or both. In the course of that period we had our share of great debates, and it is useful, as we have the beginnings of another in 1977, to think about some of them. A partial listing will be suggested to your minds, I think, by such words as Yalta, the cold war or the iron curtain, troops to Europe (a relatively specific decision which was the occasion of the first baptised Great Debate), the loss of China, liberation in Eastern Europe (a special case for Adlai Stevenson in his second campaign), atmospheric testing, in 1960 for John F. Kennedy the missile gap, for both sides in that campaign Communist Cuba 90 miles away, in 1969 the antiballistic missile, and now questions of the scale and meaning of Soviet rearmament, and such connected and important issues as human rights, symbolized specifically in senatorial debate in the Jackson Amendment. And some of these words came into the headlines two or three times, once as they were happening and once in a retrospective debate. That happened to Yalta, which was debated when it happened and reexamined some ten years later. It happened to the Cold War, debated when it began with Henry Wallace and Mr. Truman, and reexamined by historians of differing persuasions in many recent years. It happened over the fall of China where there was a debate as it happened and then a searching examination of the secretary of state who undertook to defend what had happened as no fault of the Americans. So we had more debates than there were topics, because of our tendency to debate things as they were happening and then to debate them again afterward.

A very interesting point about most of those debates, I think, is that they tended to occur in ways and at times that were not parallel either to the real points of high tension with the Russians or to the moments of formal diplomatic or political agreement with them. The real points of high tension also are worth some brief recollection:

Eastern Europe, first at the end of the war and then, in specific cases, over and over in the following twenty years and in many different ways.

Berlin twice, at the time of the blockade and then again at the end of the fifties in the crisis that was punctuated by the wall and ended by what happened in Cuba.

The Marshall Plan, where it is easy to forget that there was an extraordinarily intense and general effort of opposition mounted by the Communists and their international allies, then much more unified and vocal than they have been since.

Hungary, where the frustrations of the Americans found their outlet in a remarkably generous and effective treatment of refugees and not much more.

The missile crisis, which was certainly the largest and most dangerous but fortunately also the briefest of confrontations.

Czechoslovakia in 1968, an event clearly disappointing to Lyndon Johnson, more deeply perhaps than anything else that happened to him in international affairs, always with the exception of Vietnam, because he had committed his hopes to a place in history as the man who began the process of control of strategic arms.

The middle eastern war of 1973, a crisis that led to a general alert in very peculiar and specialized political circumstances in this country.

Angola, a crisis that aborted because the American people did not see it as a crisis.

In all this, whether it be debate or tension, I leave aside the very special and, of course, enormously important case of Vietnam because I believe it to be true that this issue, rightly or wrongly, was not governed, either in our decisions or in our debates, by attitudes toward the U.S.S.R.

The interesting point that the moments of crisis have not usually also been moments of great debate illuminates the wider reality that most of the debates have not been about immediate decisions. They have been prospective or retrospective, and it is interesting to speculate as to why that should be so. There is a small reason. From the point of view of practicing politicians it is really better to debate what has happened or what may be going to happen, and not to put one's hand on the wheel when immediate decisions are being made by others. It is less dangerous that way, and it is no criticism of the congress to say that it ordinarily proceeds in that way, except when it has become deeply disillusioned by its disapproval of a given line of conduct which has been going on for some time, or deeply hopeful about some particular prospect which has been resisted for a long time by the executive branch. Normally, in the face of something about which opinions are not yet settled, it is easier to await the event, it is easier to say "you lost China in 1950 or 1951" than it is to say, in 1948, "go save China." Although some people will say the second, many more will say the first. But there is, I think a larger reason, and one which is less conducive to cynicism, and that is that both crises and agreements (I have not listed the agreements but there were many in those twenty years, not as many as crises but enough to be important) have tended to be unifying. (There are interesting exceptions which I here leave aside.) They have tended to focus authority and support on the decision-maker. Whether the decision be for confrontation or for agreement, even in an unpleasant crisis the immediate reaction has tended to be to look to the White House. Let us take as an example, and it is an unpleasant one, the erection of the wall in Berlin in the latter part of 1961. As Americans awake on the morning after to see that the wall is there, and the question is what do you do about it, the answer can only come from one place. I worked at the White House in that period, and I remember how little advice we got on that subject in public. I don't blame anybody. We were pretty confused ourselves. Only the president could decide. He first made decisions about immediate actions of repair and encouragement. He found persons on a very wide spectrum of opinion who were willing to pitch in. General Lucius Clay and the vice-president went to encourage morale at the same time that others were enlisted to explain that this was not in fact something to go to war about, and people pitched in and helped because that was what people tended to do in the face of what was agreed to be an important, offensive, difficult phenomenon that someone had to deal with.

In retrospect it can be very different. Two kinds of retrospective thoughts appeared in the particular case of the wall. The first and most obvious was critical: Why was the U.S. government caught off base? Why didn't it know that something like this was likely to happen? Why did it have no contingency plan? Why had it not bravely sent a tank through the wall, because nobody would have started World War III over that? All these are the sorts of things that it was very easy to argue about after the moment of decision has passed. And a second retrospective view, from another perspective—equally interesting and equally little noted in the immediacy of the moment—was that cruel as the wall was, and outrageous as its murderous guards might be, something that closed the human flow from east to west was in fact the condition of any settlement of that deeply sensitive and dangerous issue. I am very far from saying that there will be no future crisis in Berlin, but I think it is at least a reasonable speculation that a settlement in Berlin could not have happened without something like the wall.

So, broadly speaking, and going back to the point that crises and agreements have tended to be unifying, what has been interesting about them is that in quite different ways (because of the different impulses they crystallize) they have tended to bring out the successful support of a public opinion that is dual—that resists Soviet pressure on the one hand and welcomes reasonable agreement on the other. And therefore, although there have been struggles over the necessary senate majorities for arms control treaties, those struggles have not been as hard as the negotiators initially thought they would be. Similarly, at moments of danger there have been questions as to whether the opinion of the country would back the government in a resolute posture, but those questions too have usually been answered affirmatively.

It has not been quite the same in the debates, so let's go back to them and, indeed, to the current debate. Like its predecessors it is mainly retrospective and prospective. It is also quite often personal and polarized, and that also is a characteristic of debate because for those who feel strongly (a minority, but usually articulate) debate is as interesting as decision, and sometimes more so. And thus you get this kind of thing (and I am not quoting, only suggesting the temper of a debate):

Q: You did take classified documents from the White House, Mr. Sorensen?

A: Yes I did, Senator. But I wrote a book that never seemed to anybody who reviewed it to say anything that they hadn't read before.

Q: But you took classified documents?

A: Yes I did.

Q: You were a conscientious objector?

A: Yes, but I said I would take the most dangerous form of noncombat service.

Q: Is it true that you opposed every weapon system recommended by the Joint Chiefs of Staff since the year 1789?

A: No, that's not quite true, Senator.

Q: Well you opposed the following thirteen?

A: Yes I did.

Q: Why do you say you merely questioned them?

A: I think questioning is a form of opposition, Senator.

Q: Well that may be your opinion.

And the argument proceeds in terms of what you have done and what maybe you will do, and what maybe you will do is even more terrifying because there we are out in the unknown at a time when some foreign power thinking about the way to win a war may encounter your naivete, and it is not good enough for you to say that in that (to you) highly hypothetical situation you would take a very tough position, because you opposed thirteen weapon systems that are the ones that would take care of this problem.

I don't want to review that recent debate in detail, and I recognize that I am not giving you a totally dispassionate account of it. I think it would be fair, however, to say that in both reading the speeches in the Congress and looking at the televised hearings it was impossible to escape the feeling that we were dealing with a debate and not a set of decisions, and with states of mind that are in some measure polarized. And I think it can be added that the processes of argumentation in the congress of the United States—especially as they developed over the long and painful years of Vietnam itself—have tended to produce a predictable polarization and that there are fewer persons in the debates who seem to be able to hold the combatants together than perhaps there were in the years of self-conscious bipartisanship that marked the early years of the Cold War.

I believe that today there is this kind of polarization and personalization in the congressional argument on many issues, not just over nominations but also over military budgets and over the particular constraints that the congress does or does not write into its legislation on matters of foreign aid and human rights and other such questions. Mostly this polarization seems less concerned with day-to-day decisions than with the expression of attitudes, but there are notable exceptions, like the congressional votes that in effect made any further intervention in Vietnam impossible and the congressional decisions that do govern the direction and flow of foreign economic assistance. Still, on the very largest questions of crisis or agreement, difference or accommodation with the Soviet Union, I think the amount of forced constriction deriving from congressional debate is still low.

Thus, I would venture to suggest to you that in the field of decision, as distinct from the field of debate, it is still correct to suppose that the initiative can belong to the executive branch. That branch is not unconstrained; its choices are delimited by two realities in our public opinion, realities demonstrated in the debates and in the events of the last thirty-five years: that there must be a real answer to any real Soviet threat to our security—that there are such things as real Soviet threats—and yet, at the same time, that good agreements are wanted. I do not think that American public opinion is incapable of holding in its collective head at one and the same time the apparently conflicting propositions that we are in all kinds of opposition to all kinds of things that the Soviet government either does or would like to do, and that at the same time our society and theirs, if they are to survive at all, must survive together. So good agreements are wanted even while threats must be countered.

The conclusion one would draw from both of these constraints is that whether it is confrontation in a crisis, or a prospect of agreement for which one needs public support against some predictable opposition, or even if it is necessary failure to agree in spite of public hopes, an administration will have to have laid its base with the American public. And in a curious way a crisis will require a preparatory base of good efforts to avoid it and an agreement will require a base of confidence that it does not endanger security. This is not a very sophisticated moral, but it is, I think, the one that you read if you look back over the record. Whether you look at debates or crises or agreements, the ones that went well had the double characteristic that the government, and in the first instance the executive branch of the government, had paid attention, before as well as during the moment of truth, to the question of public confidence with its double base of hope and fear.

So the initial prescription for the present is reasonably clear and the initial intention of the administration, as one follows it in the press, is also clear. It is right to have a more open diplomacy and to reach for much more open communication on the subjects of our foreign affairs with the American public. It is correct that there is a distance to make up here. I think this is one important reason for the particular official emphasis given to the issue of human rights in recent months. It is true that over the long course sermons from the White House are not invariably an affirmative influence on the behavior of the Soviet policy. But it is also true that when there has been conspicuous silence and indeed an articulate resistance to the direct examination of this question, it is right to even the balance because a concern for these matters is indeed intrinsic to our society. It is a part of what we believe and a part of what we wish our governments to believe, whatever they may or may not be able to do, which is an admittedly different question. I would add that as the government addresses these questions it is reasonable to hope, although there is no certainty about it, that those who take part in or judge the debates, recognizing that honest difference will continue, will think it important to be wary of what is polarized and what is personalized, what is merely retrospective or prospective. The good questions will nearly always be closely related to what we should do now, because caught as we are in the flux of time it is only now that we can speak and act.

That doesn't finish the matter. The problem, as I said at the beginning, has been complex from the start. It is not getting less so. The processes by which our relations are conducted, the issues that affect them, the other actors on the stage, the complexity of specific decisions (most obviously but not uniquely in the field of defense), all have increased, not perhaps continuously but still significantly and sometimes exponentially, over this thirty-five year period. And as you look past the personal feelings, intense as they are in the case of the Warnke hearings and debate, to the merits of the arguments made by senators on specifics of the balance of armaments and specifics of American decisions, it is not at all clear who has the better of the matter. What is clear is that we the public cannot understand the matter from merely personal arguments. When people argue about whether it is better to proceed with the conclusion of the Salt II agreement, without supplementary understandings about Backfire and the Cruise missile, I suspect that there are very few in every hundred citizens who can give even the most preliminary analysis of what those choices are. For years now I have been hearing arguments, from friends who know much more than I do, about the advantages and the disadvantages, the promise and the danger of the Cruise missile, and I have found this counsel highly inconclusive. I am convinced that we have not yet come near a solid public discussion that could lay a base for national accord on whatever the government in the end decides that it wants to do. I don't mean that the government could not get approval for a decision now, but today it would be an approval full of ignorance, and so of danger.

That danger brings me back at last to two things about this institution [MIT] and the very few that there are like it in the country or the world. I believe that the indispensable underpinning for this kind of debate is *concerned analysis,* and I would emphasize both of those words: *concerned* in the sense of both intellectual and moral care, and *analysis* in a sense that no one visiting MIT should try to expound. If there is to be general understanding on such matters, there will first have to be understanding and exposition not only by governments but by highly qualified and caring private citizens. I believe it to be true that the Massachusetts Institute of Technology, over the whole of the period I am discussing, has been clearly and continuously in the lead, often on both sides and that also is good, in the concerned analysis of both the political and the technical issues so central to this question of our relation to, and survival with, the Soviet Union. That has been an enormous contribution to the national security and to the hope of peace. It will continue so, I am sure. It is one example among many of the contributions that can be made when an institution is at once practical and philosophical, at once engaged and free. If one asserts as I do that in this enormously difficult and critical set of relations neither the national will nor the national good will has been atrophied, and if one asserts that for the next twenty years that can still be so, it must be in large part because of one's confidence in the contribution that this kind of place has made, is making, and will make.

4

Human Aggressiveness and Conflict Resolution

David A. Hamburg

I wish to begin by quoting from the remarkable background paper prepared for this series which asks the lecturers to address the question of
". . . how man might better respond to a world in which change has become rapid and pervasive as a result of the growing technological base of
society. Advances in science and technology have brought major alterations in economic, political, and military affairs and, concurrently, they
have expanded greatly the information and perceptions available to societies, affecting deep-seated patterns of culture, behavior, and expectations. Since these transformations have occurred within little more than
the working life of a single generation, it is not surprising that the world
has been unable to digest and adjust to the consequent changes. Man has
long known that he and his institutions must accommodate to change,
but our past experience has not prepared us to accommodate to such
rapid change. What is new in the present situation is that the exploitation of science and technology has so accelerated the *rate* of change of
man's condition that our traditional means for dealing with political,
economic, social, and military change are no longer adequate to the
task. The need is not only to cope with our present problems but to
develop capability to accommodate rapidly and without violence to
continuing change created by man's own actions."

The time-scale of evolution is highly relevant to contemporary human
problems. While mammals have been present on earth for more than
seventy million years, and primates appeared early among the mammals,
and a manlike form has been present for several million years, our own
species evolved to its present form only about 40,000 years ago. Agriculture has been in existence for about 10,000 years and the industrial

The research on which this paper was based was supported by The Commonwealth
Fund, The Grant Foundation, and The Harry Frank Guggenheim Foundation.

revolution occurred a mere 200 years ago. Thus, the world we live in is mainly one that we have made within the most recent phase of evolution.

The great problems of interest—such as excessive population growth, urbanization, and industrialization, with their far-reaching consequences, environmental damage and resource depletion, the nearly unimaginable risks of weapons technology—all have emerged since the industrial revolution. In a moment of evolutionary time, we have transformed the human environment—physical, biological, and social. So rapid has been this change that much of it has occurred within the memory of living adults. Yet natural selection built the human organism in ways that suited earlier environments. This process took millions of years. To a large extent, human biology (including basic behavioral tendencies) was shaped by those earlier environments. It is an open question, and a matter of concern, how well we are suited to the very new environment we have created so suddenly. In this sense we are an old species in a new habitat.

Research on evolution of behavior, especially aggressive behavior, is risky for many reasons. The clues to the past are scanty and elusive. If information is weak, authority tends to substitute for evidence. Tentative suggestions are readily assimilated to passionate political ideologies. A polemical tradition within this segment of the scientific community tends to impede rational problem-solving—though nicely illustrating once again the human capacity for rhetorical violence (as if further examples were necessary). Despite all these difficulties and more, the field has moved ahead in recent years.

Recent Research on Aggressive Behavior in Nonhuman Primates

In the course of primate (and especially of hominid) evolution, behavior has become increasingly important in adaptation. Indeed, it seems reasonable to consider that behavior is the principal means utilized by the more complex primates in maintaining relations with their environments that are conducive to survival and reproduction. The emerging field of behavior genetics has given evidence that there is abundant genetic variability underlying elementary behavior patterns.

Natural selection has presumably acted on the neural and endocrine substrates of behavior in such ways as to preserve behavioral predispositions that have, in the long run of mammalian evolution, been effective in meeting the tasks of survival and reproduction. There are some clues regarding possible mechanisms by which genes may influence neural and endocrine substrates of behavior in our own species, but this is a very young field of investigation (Hamburg, 1977; Hamburg and van Lawick-Goodall, 1974; Tanner, 1977).

Although there are different ways of formulating "natural units" of primate behavior, it is reasonable to focus attention on behavior patterns (or implicit strategies) that are utilized in several contexts: (1) obtaining food and water; (2) defending against predators; (3) defending against members of the same species; (4) mating; (5) caring for offspring; and (6) regulating temperature within the range compatible with activity requirements.

In each of these contexts, it is probable that elementary behavioral tendencies, genetically determined, are shaped by social learning experiences over the years of growth and development. To be effective in adaptation, behavior must not only take account of environmental conditions but must also coordinate the organism's physiological responses with changing external circumstances. Because of the enormous changes in the brain during primate evolution, there is a distinctive advantage for behavioral science of having animal models that are as similar to the human as possible, for both evolutionary and biomedical research. This is especially true where models of early human behavior are of interest. What can we learn about the world of our ancestors? From what baselines of behavior and environment have the recent changes taken off?

Methods of immunology and molecular biology have lately been added to traditional methods of comparing species and genera, such as comparative anatomy. This new work strengthens the traditional view that human and ape are far more similar than human and monkey. Man and the African apes are closely related, sharing a common ancestor long after the separation of apes and monkeys. The newer behavioral work also supports the close relation of African apes and our own species. I wish to speak briefly about some aspects of chimpanzee behavior because this is the species where the relationship is closest and most research has been done. In the 1960s, my colleagues and I in the Laboratory of Stress and Conflict at Stanford University chose to undertake a long-term program of research on chimpanzee behavior in an effort to obtain one useful window on the behavior of our early ancestors.

Let me make clear my view.

1. We are *not* chimpanzees.

2. We are *not descended* from chimpanzees.

3. We and they are descended from a *common ancestor,* with the separation having occurred some millions of years ago.

4. Despite this evolutionary distance between chimpanzees and ourselves, they are the closest of all living creatures to our own species (so presumptuously named *Homo sapiens*). Please bear in mind that the few remaining human hunter-gatherer societies are all composed of *Homo sapiens* and have, by and large, been severely affected by other *Homo sapiens* with more advanced weapons. So, for the student of evolution, chimpanzees are the best model of our ancestors among the nonhuman primates, whatever their limitations.

A characteristic feature of our approach has been the effort to study chimpanzee *social* behavior, in a natural habitat and in a seminatural laboratory of behavioral biology utilizing 1½ acre outdoor enclosures at Stanford. Fascinating as this may be, it is surely no substitute for studying *human* societies, and contemporary ones at that.

When studying contemporary societies, it may sometimes be useful to take into account what is known of (a) the biological nature of human organisms, and (b) the evolutionary history of human societies. Such knowledge enters into but cannot possibly substitute for direct, systematic, quantitative study of contemporary societies.

What do chimpanzees tell us about the possible origins of human agressiveness and conflict resolution? Perhaps not much—but far more than we knew a decade ago (Washburn and Hamburg, 1968). So I will sketch a few of the new findings. But first a word of background.

Chimpanzees live in societies that are very complex by nonhuman primate standards, probably similar in important respects to the societies of early man (Australopithecus) but dramatically smaller and simpler than twentieth-century human societies. There are about forty animals in a community, spread over about fifteen to twenty square miles of forest, walking and climbing miles per day in the food quest, subsisting mainly by gathering plants but also hunting small mammals whenever the opportunity arises. They interact with each other in predictable ways, apparently following implicit rules which they learn during the long years of growth and development. These rules cover conditions under which threat, attack, submissive, and reassurance patterns occur and the signals useful in their termination (van Lawick-Goodall, 1968; van Lawick-Goodall, 1971).

The early phase of observations at Gombe National Park in Tanzania in the 1960s were useful in the habituation of the animals to human observers; description of behavioral components; building a history of individual relationships, especially in regard to kinship; stimulating interest in and demonstrating the feasibility of research on great apes.

When this phase was completed, a gradual change in research methods was essential for further progress: (1) the construction of an interdisciplinary group to bring fresh perspectives to bear on chimpanzee behavior; (2) a shift from general description to problems with a relatively sharp focus; (3) extensive following of individuals beyond the "camp" area (where provisioning occurred) to the far recesses of the forest, eventually covering the entire range of the study population; (4) recording data in the systematic way in specified categories of behavior and, insofar as possible under the circumstances, taking a quantitative approach to the data; (5) systematically sampling of each age/sex class; (6) observing interactions between different communities and subcommunities. Utilization of these new methods in the 1970–1975 period inevitably extended earlier findings, modified some, and led to their reformulation.

Until very recently the observations of chimpanzees in natural habitats were almost entirely within-community behavior. Now we have data on between-community interactions. These observations provide one of the most striking examples of the changes that have occurred in understanding of chimpanzee social behavior as a result of more systematic and long-term studies (Bygott, in press; Nishida, in press). Reports on chimpanzee social organization in the 1960s suggested that there were no discernable social units above the level of a mother and her offspring and that chimpanzees moved freely about the forest, now and then peacefully interacting with whomever they encountered. The new data on intercommunity contact deviates dramatically from earlier idyllic notions of chimpanzee life: chimpanzee males are organized into distinct communities which occupy ranges that are defended against males from other communities. When males from different communities come into contact, violent fights may occur and individuals are sometimes severely injured. Perhaps even more surprising is the fact that females and infants are not immune to violent aggression by males from other communities.

Moreover, several studies establish the patrolling of community boundaries by groups of males who behave in distinctive (chiefly antagonistic)

ways in such encounters. Males from a given community not only attempt to defend the community range when they happen to hear or encounter males from other communities, but they actively seek out such
encounters during forays labelled "patrols." Although females, usually
females in sexually receptive condition, sometimes accompany males on
"patrols," they rarely take an active part in actual intercommunity encounters. While most aggressive encounters between communities involve
males, females from other communities are also sometimes severely at-
tacked, and in three cases infants have been killed during such attacks.

What is the function of such intercommunity aggression? Some workers
have suggested that, by defending community range boundaries, a group
of males achieves access to a greater number of females and other resources. The main difference between male territorial systems in other
mammals and in chimpanzees is that the larger chimpanzee territory appears to be established and defended by groups of males cooperating
with one another, whereas in other species single males defend areas from
all other males. In general, there is evidence that the evolution of cooper-
ative behavior is related to the evolution of aggressive behavior in primates.

In a valuable new paper, Nishida (in press) gives an overview of years of
research on wild chimpanzees at a different location in Tanzania. There is
an impressive conjunction of findings between these investigators and the
Gombe group. Increasing evidence at both locations indicates that communities of thirty to fifty individuals tend to be quite distinct from each
other, though not totally impermeable. The members of different communities usually tend to avoid each other, and smaller groups give way to
larger groups when they meet. Relatively severe aggression tends to occur
when members of different communities come into close contact, mainly
involving adult males. These communities appear to have well-delineated,
traditional boundaries over a seven-year period.

Behavior of chimpanzees in the Mahali Mountains closely resembles the
"patrolling" behavior of chimpanzees at Gombe. Fascinating though these
observations are, we must be cautious in relating this new information on
intercommunity hostility to the possible evolutionary roots of human
warfare.

These new observations of free-living chimpanzees by two independent
groups of investigators conducting careful, longitudinal studies considerably strengthen the concept that stranger-contact is a powerful instigator
of aggressive behavior in higher primates (Hamburg, 1971). The concept
encompasses relative strangeness involving individuals who have con-

siderable familiarity with each other but are separated sufficiently in time or space to heighten the probability of aggression upon contact.

This concept applies to within-community behavior as well. Indeed, it has even been studied in a quasi-experimental way in the wild and in laboratory settings.

The crowding of strangers in the presence of valued resources appears to constitute a set of conditions conducive to serious aggression among nonhuman primates. Note that crowding alone does not seem to have a powerful effect, but crowding relative strangers in the presence of valued resources is another story. In the early years of the work at Gombe, Goodall arranged for the provision of bananas as a dietary supplement in a small cleared area of forest. This situation has now been systematically studied by Wrangham (Wrangham, 1974) over a period of years during which the availability of bananas was raised to a high level and then decreased to a low level. He found that the attractiveness of the bananas drew unusually large aggregations of chimpanzees into this small area, some of whom probably had relatively little contact with each other in other circumstances. During this period there was a high frequency of aggressive interactions among chimpanzees and also between chimpanzees and baboons. With the decline of banana feeding in subsequent years there was less crowding, two subgroups of adult males withdrew from each other, and aggressive interactions became less frequent in the banana area.

I do not want to leave you with the impression that this is the only or even the principal eliciting condition for threat and attack behavior in higher primates. The main within-community precipitating factors for aggression are as follows:

1. in daily transactions involving status or dominance;
2. in long-term changes of status or dominance, especially among males (adolescence is of special interest here);
3. in frustration with animals of similar or higher status, precipitating aggression toward a lower status individual (redirection);
4. in the protection of infants by adults of both sexes, but especially by females;
5. in defending against potential predators;
6. in killing and eating young animals of other species;
7. in terminating severe disputes among subordinate animals;
8. in association with a presumably painful injury;
9. in the exploration of strange or dangerous areas;
10. in meeting relatively unfamiliar animals;

11. in circumstances where highly valued resources are in short supply; and
12. in circumstances where relatively strange animals are crowded in the presence of highly valued resources.

An Evolutionary Perspective on Human Aggression

The observations of aggressive behavior in higher primates deserve consideration in the framework of an adaptive evolutionary view of aggressive behavior. Although we cannot be sure of the ways in which aggressive behavior has functioned adaptively during the course of evolution, the following possibilities deserve serious consideration: (a) increasing the means of defense; (b) providing access to valued resources such as food, water, and females in reproductive condition; (c) contributing to effective utilization of the habitat by distributing animals in relation to available resources; (d) resolving serious disputes within the group; (e) providing a predictable social environment; (f) providing leadership for the group, particularly in dangerous circumstances; and finally (g) differential reproduction. It is plausible (though not proved) that relatively aggressive males are more likely to pass on their genes to subsequent generations than less aggressive males.

Some of these factors may have given selective advantage to aggressive primates, if they could effectively regulate their aggressive behavior. Primates do have well defined cues that usually terminate aggressive sequences and an elaborate repertoire of submissive behavior. Most of the time they have a stable dominance hierarchy that contributes to the predictability of the social environment, and they have clear sequences of aggression-submission-reassurance that have elements in common with human behavior. Future research will profit from paying as much attention to the regulation and control of aggressive tendencies as to their sources and instigation.

The adaptability of aggressive behavior in past environments gives no assurance whatever that similar behavior would function adaptively in the very different environment of contemporary man. Scholars differ as to the fate of primate aggressive tendencies during the two to three million years that man has lived in hunting-and-gathering societies, but there is reason to believe that tendencies of this sort were strengthened by the advent of agriculture and permanent settlements about 10,000 years ago. Such heightening of aggressiveness may well be a matter only

of social expression, not genetic change. But it may also reflect changing selection pressures that modified the basic nature of the human organism. However that may be, the rich historical record is replete with suspicion, hatred, and violence; and the advent of complex weapons technology has suddenly and drastically escalated the risks of such behavior.

Overall, research of recent years on primate behavior has decreased the gap between human and nonhuman primates, especially chimpanzees. Among the similarities, one of the most intriguing is the enduring quality of attachments in the higher primates, especially those of chimpanzees and of humans. Attachment between chimpanzee mothers and their offspring, and between siblings, may last throughout the life span. Such relationships provide mutual support under stress, joint access to vital resources, and models for learning adaptive behavior. The role of behavior in adaptation is not only a function of individuals but of groups as well. This is strikingly true of higher primates. Both nonhuman primates and early humans have been organized into small societies. These societies provide, first, intimate, enduring relationships with mutual assistance in difficult circumstances; and second, clear guidelines for individual behavior, highly relevant to survival requirements in a given environment.

Recent studies of human infants have suggested processes by which emotionally charged and enduring attachments are formed in early life.

There has probably been an evolutionary premium on the capacity to form attachments because of their adaptive utility in the line that led to *Homo sapiens* (Hamburg, 1963). Human groups can usefully be viewed as pools of potential attachments. This attachment pool manifested itself in somewhat different ways in different evolutionary eras, but always there was a small core group of well-known individuals, some of whom were ready at a moment's notice to be helpful. These considerations apply to the millions of years in which some nonhuman primates were slowly evolving in the hominid direction; to the several million years in which hominids were organized in hunting-and-gathering societies of thirty to fifty people, extended somewhat by kinship relations with neighboring bands; to the extended family of agricultural village society; and to the primary group of the homogeneous neighborhood in preindustrial towns.

These small groups must have shaped the world of human perceptions, beliefs, and values. Such groups can so well provide the security of thorough familiarity with the environment, support in times of stress, clearcut guidelines for behavior, and enduring attachments throughout the life span. These are assets highly valued by humans everywhere. Yet other

emotionally charged values have modified these circumstances in the twentieth century in a way that must be largely unprecedented in human evolution (Hamburg, 1975).

Two implications of this observation deserve more than the brief mention I can give them here: (1) it is very difficult to shift from the small, face-to-face, fairly stable, clear-cut society of our long evolutionary history to the immensely complicated, vast, heterogeneous society that has burst upon us in a moment of evolutionary time, (2) much of human aggression is in the service of attachment. We risk our lives, kill our enemies, ravage the planet in the commitment to those we care about. In the name of love and duty and brotherhood, we carry out the threats and attacks that now constitute the ultimate peril to our species.

It is reasonable to suppose that nonhuman and human primate societies have been meeting the adaptive requirements of their populations for millions of years, varying their behavior in accordance with the environmental conditions they had to meet. Individuals have been prepared throughout a lengthy childhood for their roles in a particular social system. In effect, each social system gives instructions on ways of meeting specific adaptive tasks.

When the environment was largely stable in evolution over long periods of time, guidelines for behavior emerged that were broadly useful in meeting adaptive tasks. Many guidelines for behavior were taught early in life, shaped by powerful rewards and punishments, invested with strong emotions supported by social norms.

In many species early learning of guidelines for adaptive behavior tends to induce lifelong commitments. Over long time-spans, these emotionally charged guidelines tend to prepare the young to meet the adaptive requirements of the environment by fulfilling the roles of adult life—that is, effective ways in particular circumstances of meeting the problems of survival and reproduction. Much of hominid evolution has been characterized by frequent subsistence uncertainties and occasional threats of natural disaster. Vulnerability to environmental vicissitudes was a constant feature of life for our ancestors. Thus, technology that could enhance man's control of the environment has been historically attractive. In light of basic survival concerns, technology has often been pursued vigorously and has sometimes transformed society. Such transformations occurred at the time of the industrial revolution, again between 1870 and 1900 in the face of an acceleration in science and technology, and most recently in the years since World War II. On the time scale of evolution these are very recent changes, and their rate is exceedingly rapid.

In times of such rapid technological and social change, old guidelines for behavior tend to become uncertain or discredited in some sectors of society, yet they persist in others. Such behavioral guidelines refer to human relationships, to relations with the physical environment, and to meeting problems of life and death. Long-established guidelines may be poorly suited to new conditions, but if they have worked well for long periods they are difficult to change. The difficulty in changing such behavior patterns is related to fundamental motivations that have long been relevant to survival. Behaving according to established guidelines supports a sense of personal worth and a sense of belonging in valued groups. Some dimensions of culture may change much more rapidly than others— for example, a drastic technological change may disrupt the established way of life whose values and institutions may lag behind, poignantly devoted to emotionally charged traditions that arose in earlier and perhaps quite different circumstances. But the need for change in behavior is actually greatest when drastic environmental changes are occurring. In evolution, these are the times of maximum risk for species extinction.

Some years ago, I suggested that there is likely to be a special facility for learning in directions that have been valuable for the species over a very long time in evolution (Hamburg, 1963). For any species, some patterns of behavior are easy to learn, some difficult, and some impossible. Learning in such adaptively significant spheres as those concerned with food, water, and reproduction has probably had high biological priority; and aggression can serve in the implementation of these adaptive requirements. If this is on the right trail, then we might expect the human brain to be organized in ways that reflect the long-term selective advantage of facility in learning such behavior. Simple preferences on the part of the infant or young child might draw his attention to a certain class of stimuli, or reward his engagement in a particular kind of activity—for example, rough-and-tumble play. Once drawn in this direction early in life by an inherited preference, complex learning could ensue, taking full account of cultural preferences and parental guidance.

The biological equipment of the contemporary human organism is derived from environmental conditions long since gone or outmoded. Some of our emotional response tendencies and learning orientations, mediated by the old limbric-hypothalamic-midbrain circuits, were probably built into the machine because they worked well in its adaptation over many thousands or even millions of years. There has been very little time for change in biological structure since the industrial revolution began two centuries ago. But the conditions of life are very different now than then, and the power at our disposal, for better or worse, is incredibly greater.

Popular writers on the subject of human aggressiveness tend to dichotomize into two schools: (1) the human is a sinner, a savage beast, a no-longer-naked and now heavily armed ape who will surely destroy himself and his planet; and (2) the human is a saint, inherently good and tender and loving, corrupted only by corrupting societies, behaving aggressively only under extreme provocation. My own view is more complex: human is saint and sinner and much more.

Even the saintly school admits there is an elaborate apparatus of neural circuitry, neurochemistry, and neuroendocrinology that mediates human aggressive behavior. The underlying mechanisms are being elucidated in current research by such distinguished investigators as MIT's own Walle Nauta and Richard Wurtman. This is not the occasion for discussing the biological mechanisms of aggression; but progress is being made and can be followed in the new journal *Aggressive Behavior*. Also, progress in related disciplines of behavioral science is being made and deserves attention (Daniels et al., 1970; Deutsch, 1973).

Conflicts in Contemporary Societies and Paths Toward Resolution

We are now in a position to appreciate the enormity of the transition in which we have lived our lives. For instance, there are now more working scientists than there had been in all of history put together up until a few decades ago. Multiply this example by a thousand or even a million and we can realize how suddenly we have been thrust into a world of enormous complexity, heterogeneity, cross-cutting interests, diverse pressures, and unimaginable weapons. Our power for better or worse, suddenly dwarfs all of history. This power is, above all, significant in relation to our conflict-laden history as a species. But is conflict still an important feature of our lives? Is it possible that serious conflict is now merely an occasional aberration of peculiar circumstances? If so, we could more promptly modify or avoid those circumstances.

In historical times conflict between groups has been and continues to be common, often destructive, and varied in content. Yet there are widely shared properties in the form of such antagonisms. Human societies have a pervasive tendency to make distinctions between good and bad people, between in-groups and out-groups. This sorting tendency is very widespread, readily learned, and susceptible to harsh dichotomizing between positively valued "we" and negatively valued "they."

Hostility between human groups is likely to arise when the groups perceive a conflict of vital interests, an unacceptable difference in status, or a difference of beliefs that jeopardizes self-esteem. Such situations tend to evoke sharp in-group, out-group solidarity, with drastic depreciation of the out-group by the in-group. Perceived threat from an out-group tends to enhance in-group solidarity, tightness of group boundaries, and punishment of those who deviate from group norms. (They seem readily able to find a threatening group. Tyrants have understood this for centuries.)

Justification for harming out-group members rests on sharp distinctions between "we" and "they," between good people and bad people. Such justification is readily provided by assumptions regarding (1) the damage they would do to the in-group ("what we do is in self-defense"); (2) the damage they would inadvertently do to themselves ("we must protect them"); and (3) classification of the out-group as essentially non-human ("pseudo-speciation").

Many different political, social, economic, and pseudo-scientific ideologies may be mobilized in support of these hostile positions. Although the content of such intergroup hostility varies widely from time to time and from place to place, the form is remarkably similar. Such antagonisms have been studied by social scientists and referred to as "ethnocentrism" (Levine and Campbell, 1972). It is easy to put ourselves at the center of the universe, attaching a strong positive value to one's self and one's group, while attaching a negative value to many other people and their groups. Since these patterns are not limited to ethnic groups, a term like "groupocentrism" is more appropriate. Groups have in fact been specified not only by ethnicity but by religion, race, language, region, tribe, nation, and various political entities. The same principles seem to apply across different kinds of groups. Can human groups achieve internal cohesion, self-respect, and adaptive effectiveness without promoting hatred and violence? A deeper understanding of factors that influence groupocentrism could have much practical value in resolving intergroup conflicts. In my judgment this is a crucial area for scientific effort. Here as elsewhere, changes in human circumstances have been so rapid that traditional responses have been inadequate. In this instance policymakers and scientists have not, until very recently, thought of these problems as suitable for scientific study, and only a very modest investment has been made in such research.

Let us consider a change in psychological orientation—coming to think of ourselves as a single species, identifying ourselves with the entire species on a worldwide basis, and doing so in a way that respects diversity. If we recognize common properties of a worldwide species, we nevertheless recognize, respect, and to some extent understand diversity within that species—diversity not only in terms of individuals on a biological basis but diversity in terms of cultural traditions and social organizations. Perhaps the extended family could provide a model for the human family in a larger sense. This is a very difficult psychological problem. Through most of human history a small number of people have been highly significant for each individual, have been deeply meaningful to the individual, have constituted the individual's enduring attachments. Perhaps we can broaden that perspective to take seriously the welfare of a great many individuals spread through a worldwide community. It will not be easy to do so.

Now let us consider superordinate goals. On this point, the landmark in behavioral science research is Sherif's Robbers' Cave experiment in which he showed that young boys who had been in two conflicting groups were brought into harmony only when they were faced with a superordinate goal—that is, a goal that was very important to both groups and could only be attained by their joint effort. In practical terms we are faced with the serious question: What, if anything, can constitute a compelling superordinate goal for large groups of human beings organized over vast distances in mutually suspicious societies? Perhaps the clear and present danger to survival inherent in atomic weapons provides one such goal. To say the least, the advent of atomic weapons suggests the possibility that we must work together in order to avoid extinction as a species, or at least to avoid destruction of our present cultures. We have now lived in the shadow of extinction for about three decades, but world leaders still tend to speak in nineteenth-century terms. The public tends to avoid thinking about such dangers which are inherently distressing when squarely faced. Most individuals and small groups feel a sense of helplessness in the face of such risks and tend automatically to avoid thinking about them. It is not yet clear whether we have come to perceive the atomic risks as a fundamental superordinate goal requiring the cooperation of diverse groups for survival. Perhaps the time scale is too short for such an appraisal.

More recently, another possibility has arisen: biological warfare. Could this survival risk become an effective superordinate goal? In this decade there has been growing recognition of the possibility that biological warfare could not be safely managed. Scientists in various countries have been effective in clarifying the concept that a new and uncontrollable menace to the species might arise, and this understanding seems to have contributed to promising agreements that have been reached. By the same token there has been encouraging, though limited, agreement in respect to atomic weapons. It is my impression that persuasive activity by distinguished scientists, in part through the mass media, has helped to create some sense of cooperation for survival as a superordinate goal in respect to atomic and biological warfare.

Another possible superordinate goal has grown markedly in public attention during this decade: irreversible damage to the environment. There is a growing scientific literature on problems of serious ecological disruption related to rapid population growth, increasing technological complexity, environmental pollution, and resource depletion. This set of threats to survival, which we may well call an ecological crisis, could come to be appraised on a worldwide basis as a superordinate goal requiring cooperation for survival; but this has not yet come to pass. One recalls the beautiful photograph of tiny earth seen from the moon—surely one of the most valuable contributions of the space program. How vivid our interdependence!

We come now to the topic of overlapping group memberships. Where multiple loyalties exist, rather than single-minded loyalty to one group only, it becomes possible to link peoples of quite different groups together. Leaders of population groups with overlapping multiple loyalties can become effective bridging persons in time of stress and conflict. International organizations can function similarly. I refer here not only to governmental organizations but to professional and scientific societies, commercial organizations, and other groups that function effectively across cultures. Other examples come to mind: Peace Corps; youth organizations; exchange missions, especially if frequently repeated over extended time. At the very least, such organizations can promote personal contact and tend to diminish stereotypes; perhaps in the long run, on a large scale, such multiple loyalties can become strong enough to exert a restraining influence on international hostilities. Overlapping loyalties that cut across traditional in-group, out-group antagonisms are particularly significant. Studies of community conflict have revealed the problem-solving potential of intermediary associations through which opinions may be expressed, the common humanity of the adversaries kept in mind on both sides, and plausible compromises gradually sorted out.

There is a great need for organized, visible, skilled reconciliation services in respect to the whole range of intergroup conflict. Indeed it seems likely that one or more high-level professions may emerge over the next decade or two devoted entirely to mobilizing the maximum possible competence in fair, objective, agreed-upon procedures for resolving disputes. A considerable body of relevant experience has arisen, such as in labor-management relations. But educational and research efforts in this field have, for the most part, been inadequate to the needs and the opportunities.

I turn now to the enormous possibilities, for better or worse, opened up by the new technology of television in respect to human conflict. But first a word of background from research on the learning of aggressive patterns.

Observational learning in a social context, learning by viewing models, has been understood in recent years as an important mode of adaptation in nonhuman primates. It is an important mode of learning for human infants and children as well: observations of the mass media, observations of parents, siblings, peers, and leaders. So the attractive models available during the years of growth and development have much bearing on the learning of intergroup relations. The model says to the child, in effect, "if you're frustrated, here is what to do," or, in a broad sense, "if survival is threatened, this is what you should do." Viewed in this way, there is a linkage between biological orientations, frustration patterns, models, and cultural norms. Attractive models of violence link with cultural norms.

Children and adolescents learn much about violent responses to other groups from culturally prominent models, for instance, by watching television. There is no need here to review the evidence relating televised violence with the propensity to behave violently in play and probably in real life as well. The prime time violence may have declined slightly in the past few years but remains at exceedingly high levels in this country. Moreover, the violence is generally "sanitized"; that is, done in what is called "good taste." This means that the odious consequences of violence are not usually shown. To a large extent, violence is vividly presented as an effective way of solving problems. The source of difficulty is removed in a way that is often attractive in terms of bravery or boldness or skill; so, the cultural norm as reflected in the mass media is frequent violence with the clear implication that violence is useful, commonplace, and often admirable.

Studies of American television show that the cumulative exposure is very large indeed. In our population children spend roughly the same amount of time watching television as in attending school. There is some research evidence suggesting that television need not be a school for violence but can indeed be used in a way that reduces intergroup hostility. I hope a high priority will be attached to the constructive use of this powerful tool to promote compassionate understanding, nonviolent problem-solving, and decent intergroup relations. Of all the technological advances of the twentieth century, I suppose none is more important for the future of our species than television; a genuine evolutionary novelty. It is a worldwide, instantaneous, comprehensible network with high emotional impact. It can link different groups, different cultures, indeed the entire planet, as never before. But its potential for reducing intergroup conflict has scarcely been utilized so far. Television can vividly portray group diversity sympathetically while highlighting shared human experiences—the understanding and compassionate appraisal of common human experiences across subcultural differences and cultural variations on basic adaptive themes—including the common humanity of our adversaries, even in times of stress.

Indeed, education in all its forms—from family through schools to mass media—must increasingly come to appreciate and convey the facts of an exceedingly complex, pluralistic, crowded, interdependent, and fascinating world. Education must be broadened in its channels and its content to convey around the world the indelible image of a single species, a huge family including many cousins, more similar than otherwise, groping for a decent life chances in many ways, necessarily relying for survival on the give-and-take we learn in childhood—now extended far beyond our childhood games.

To speak of such matters, and especially of the uses of television, must surely make us think of leadership. Indeed, the principal link between individual human behavior (including aggressiveness) and the immensely dangerous conflicts between powerfully armed nations, is to be found in the behavior of leaders. Although I refer here principally to political leaders, the concepts I wish to discuss apply similarly to leaders in education, science, and industry.

Some Ways of Enhancing the Conflict-Resolving Capacities of Leaders

For some years, I have had the privilege of working with Alexander George, Professor of Political Science at Stanford. Our interests converge on problems of decision-making under stress in a variety of contexts. One of these contexts is leadership in crisis involving high risk of conflict escalation. In the remarks that follow, I rely heavily on his scholarly work and that of his colleagues, especially in regard to a recent volume prepared for the Commission on the Organization of the Government for the Conduct of Foreign Policy (Appendixes, vol. 2, 1975). Political decision makers typically operate under the following limitations: (1) incomplete information about the situation; (2) inadequate knowledge of the relation between ends and means, with the consequence that the leader cannot predict with high confidence the consequences of choosing a given course of action; and (3) difficulty in formulating a single criterion for use in choosing the best available option. In such a setting, strategies for dealing with cognitive complexity become essential. The leader who cannot tolerate complexity is likely to be a dangerous leader. These difficult situations typically pose multiple stakes for the decision maker that cannot readily be reconciled. A national leader must consider his national interest (often employing an unduly restrictive, indeed obsolete, concept of what constitutes national interest); he must also often weigh the interests of his political group, passionate interest groups, and the lives of many unknown individuals whose voices are faintly heard—not to speak of his own family and his sense of worth as a person. In principle, the leader can today elicit more relevant information and more potent analytical capabilities than ever before. And we must find ways to enhance those capacities further. But as we know from painful experience, these potentialities for effective problem-solving seem rarely to work as we hope. We must learn more about ways in which the potentiality of reasonable, well-informed decision-making can actually be achieved in difficult real-life circumstances.

A major theme in the analysis of both small advisory groups and the larger organizational context in which leaders make decisions has to do with the strong advantages of explicitly considering a wide range of alternatives, including unpleasant ones, before making a major decision. An important line of inquiry that has practical bearing on such decisions as those of Vietnam and Watergate is to clarify the factors in small groups and large organizations that tend either to inhibit or to facilitate a consideration of multiple alternatives. There are fundamental advantages of planning procedures that encourage critical, broadgauged consideration of many overlapping and competing factors that are embedded in a particular problem. In so doing, alternative courses of action can be formulated with increasing clarity, and the advantages and limitations of each can then be assessed in a way that draws upon the best available evidence, involving not only protection of the decision maker's sense of worth but also giving serious consideration to the multiple stakes at issue (Coelho, Hamburg, and Adams, 1975).

But many institutional arrangements and semiperpetual crisis atmospheres do not foster such rational problem-solving. We must pay attention to organizational interventions that can systematically strengthen a leader's problem-solving capacity. For example, leaders need organizational early warning systems. Because it is so difficult under most stressful circumstances to make anything like an optimal decision, there is an urgent need for monitoring the course of the transaction with the environment in such a way as to detect untoward consequences as they are beginning to appear, but before irreversible damage has occurred.

George has identified from recent historical cases some factors that increase the risk of malfunction in the decision-making processes. These malfunctions tend to occur under the following conditions: (1) when the decision maker and his advisors agree too readily on the nature of the problem and on a single response to it; (2) when advisors take up alternatives with the decision maker, but cover only a narrow range of options; (3) when there is no advocate for an unpopular option; (4) when advisors work out their own disagreements over alternative possibilities without the decision maker's knowledge and then present him with a single recommendation; (5) when advisors agree privately among themselves that the decision maker should face up to a distressing situation, but no one is willing to alert him to it; (6) when the decision maker is largely dependent upon a single channel of information; (7) when the underlying assumptions of a plan have been evaluated only by the advocates of that option; (8) when the decision maker does not arrange for a well-qualified group to examine carefully the negative judgment offered by a critic or devil's advocate on a course of action preferred by the leader; and (9) when the decision-maker is impressed by a consensus among his advisors but does not thoroughly examine the adequacy of its basis. Making explicit these sources of interference with effective problem solving will enhance opportunities for coping with stressful decision-making situations that affect the crucial conflicts of our time.

Several recent and forthcoming publications elucidate this approach in some detail, with data and theory from psychological and social research related to some of the principal leadership decisions of the twentieth century. These include contributions by Alexander George (1975), Robert Jervis (1976), Irving Janis, and Leon Mann (1977). However dimly seen, the shape of better institutional arrangements is becoming visible—

arrangements that can come closer than we are now to maximizing the rational, problem-solving capacity of leaders in the context of humane and compassionate values.

The quest for social justice, so far poorly fulfilled, is a deep and recurrent theme in human conflicts. It is an economic problem, to be sure, but more, much more. It is a matter of human dignity and decency, sharing and stimulation, compassion and understanding, the appreciation of diversity, and respect for an almost endless variety of ecological niches in which people find their satisfactions.

The poignant dilemma is that ways of fostering survival, self-esteem, close human relationships, and meaningful group membership for hundreds, thousands, or even millions of years now often turn out to be ineffective or even dangerous in the new world in which we find ourselves. Some of the old ways are still useful, others are not. They will have to be sorted out as carefully as we can. Where old ways are no longer suitable, new ways must be found that are more suitable for the changed conditions of contemporary life.

The intimate slowly changing world of the nonhuman primates and of early man is gone now and gone forever. So, too, is the small and simple world of agrarian society. Our world is the new, large, crowded, heterogeneous, impersonal, rapidly changing world of the past two centuries. There is little in our history as a species to prepare us for this world we have made.

To meet this crucial set of tasks will require the mobilization of the sciences over their entire range. This bicentennial series suggests to me that MIT will provide leadership. Other institutions of science and higher education must join. Attitudes, emotions, beliefs, and political ideologies from our past will often hinder such efforts to enhance our understanding and even impede the utilization of scientific knowledge when it is available. But our motivation for survival is strong, our problem-solving capacities are great, and the time is not yet too late.

In respect to the resolution of conflicts—and the more equitable distribution of resources—it is the difficult task of contemporary humans to invent solutions to problems that are largely unprecedented in the history of the species. Science can help—probably help a great deal. But to be truly effective in meeting these extraordinary human predicaments, science too must transcend its traditional boundaries and achieve a level of mutual understanding, innovation, and cooperation among its disciplines rarely achieved in the past.

References

Bygott, J.D. (in press) "Agonistic behavior and dominance among wild chimpanzees." In *Behavior of Great Apes,* eds. D. A. Hamburg and E. McCown. Menlo Park: W. A. Benjamin.

Coelho, G. V., Hamburg, D. A., and Adams, J. E., eds. 1974. *Coping and Adaptation.* New York: Basic Books, Inc.

Commission on the Organization of the Government for the Conduct of Foreign Policy. 1975. Appendices, vol. 2. Washington, D.C.: U.S. Government Printing Office.

Daniels, D. N., Gilula, M. F. and Ochberg, F. M., eds. 1970. *Violence and the Struggle for Existence,* p. 441, Boston: Little, Brown.

Deutsch, M. 1973. *The Resolution of Conflict: Constructive and Destructive Processes,* p. 420, New Haven: Yale University Press.

George, Alexander L. 1974. "Adaptation to stress in political decision making: the individual, small group, and organizational contexts." In *Coping and Adaptation,* G. V. Coelho, D. A. Hamburg, and J. E. Adams, eds. New York: Basic Books, Inc.

Hamburg, D. A. 1963. "Emotions in the perspective of human evolution." In *Expressions of the Emotions in Man,* ed. P. Knapp, p. 300. New York: International Universities Press.

———. 1971. "Crowding, stranger contact, and aggressive behavior." In *Stress, Society and Disease,* ed. L. Levi, p. 209. New York: Oxford University Press.

———. 1975. "Ancient man in the twentieth century." In *The Quest for Man,* ed. Vanne Goodall. London: Phaidon Press Ltd.

———. 1977. "Developments in research on the psychobiology of aggression." In *Developments in Psychiatric Research,* J. M. Tanner, ed. London: Hodder & Stoughton.

———and van Lawick-Goodall, J. 1974. "Factors facilitating development of aggressive behavior in chimpanzee and humans." In *Determinants and Origins of Aggressive Behavior,* eds. W. W. Hartup and J. deWit, p. 57. The Hague: Mouton.

Janis, I. L. and Mann, L. 1977. *Decision Making: A Psychological Analysis of Conflict, Choice, and Commitment.* New York: The Free Press.

Jervis, Robert. 1976. *Perception and Misperception in International Politics,* Princeton, New Jersey: Princeton University Press.

Levine, R. and Campbell, D. 1972. *Ethnocentrism, Theories of Conflict, Ethnic Attitudes and Group Behavior,* p. 310, New York: Wiley.

Nishida, T. (in press) "The social structure of chimpanzees of the Mahali mountains." In *Behavior of Great Apes,* eds. D. A. Hamburg and E. McCown. Menlo Park: W. A. Benjamin.

van Lawick-Goodall, J. 1968. "A preliminary report on expressive movements and communication in the Gombe Stream chimpanzees." In *Primates: Studies in Adaptation and Variability,* ed. P. C. Jay, p. 313. New York: Holt, Rinehart and Winston.

———. 1971. Some aspects of aggressive behaviour in a group of free-living chimpanzees. *International Social Science Journal,* 23, 89–97.

Washburn, S. L. and Hamburg, D. A. 1968. Aggressive behavior in old-world monkeys and apes. In *Primates: Studies in Adaptation and Variability,* ed. P. C. Jay, p. 458, New York: Holt, Rinehart and Winston.

Wrangham, R. W. 1974. "Artificial feeding of chimpanzees and baboons in their natural habitat." *Animal Behavior,* 22, 83–93.

5

Critical Decisions
in Relation to Energy

Sigvard Eklund

At the outset I would like to define what I mean by the topic "Critical Decisions in Relation to Energy." I refer not only to decisions that face governments (your own government is now in the process of evolving a comprehensive energy policy) but to decisions that face every individual. The outcome may not only have a bearing on world security, but will certainly affect societal changes, and may indeed determine whether society, as we know it today, will survive.

During the last five years an enormous number of studies, some superficial, some penetrating, have been made on the demand and supply of energy, whether on a national or global basis. Though the subject seemingly achieved instant popularity at the time of the 1973 "energy crisis," the problems involved have been and will continue to be with us for a long time. Let me recall what Mr. Schlesinger, the president's adviser on energy matters, said: "The energy crisis is just beginning." Predictably, each energy "crunch" elicits a series of new studies and strategies. Yet, decisions taken are almost without exception based on short-term criteria. My purpose is to discuss some of the decisions that must or should be taken to ensure an orderly utilization, on a long-term basis, of the resources required to provide the energy for tomorrow's needs. These decisions will, for the most part, be taken by national authorities within a national context. They require, however, an appreciation of the global situation and in many instances a great deal of international cooperation.

I have just seen the report of the Nuclear Energy Policy Study Group with Spurgeon M. Keeny as chairman, sponsored by the Ford Foundation and administered by the Mitre Corporation. The report gives the impression of an objective and thorough evaluation of the energy situation and the role nuclear energy can play in the United States and the world. I have, however, the feeling that the conclusions mainly take account of conditions in the United States whereas different situations in other parts of the world may not have been fully considered.

To what degree will the changing world affect the energy situation? "Change" in industrialized countries has been associated with progress, which, in turn, implies expansion and growth. Since energy, until recently, was considered to be an abundant and cheap commodity, its availability was assumed. The main question has been that of how to use it to achieve more speed, more comfort, more rapid communication and greater industrial development. Electricity has responded particularly well to our demands and has supplied more and more of the energy requirements. However, when the price of oil, which accounts for close to half of the world's energy consumption, was more than quadrupled within three months following a temporary embargo in 1973, a number of questions began to plague decision makers. Such questions as: What is the extent of presently usable energy resources (oil, gas, coal, hydro, uranium) and how are they distributed world-wide? How much of these resources, and at what price, can a nation afford to import? To what extent can political factors affect supplies? If access to energy sources is threatened and national security jeopardized, what measures at what cost can be taken to cut down demand? What kind of a society and what patterns of consumption should we strive for, given limited and expensive sources of energy?

I do not propose to address all of these issues, but limit myself to the consideration of the following questions: first, the need for energy growth; second, energy resources presently available to man; third, short- and long-term alternatives; and, fourth, the pros and cons of the various alternatives now available to us. I will also touch on the question of nuclear proliferation.

First, do we need any energy growth at all? This may seem a rather strange question after the experiences of past winters, and I do not think an empirical answer is possible. What recent events have shown is that a shortage of energy, or a sharp rise in its price, affects poor countries and poor people hardest. In a more affluent society the value of an additional unit of energy may be marginal, but for the poor it may represent an extra bowl of rice, a gallon of water, light in the darkness, better sanitation, or a warm room. Energy conservation in such circumstances is another term for hardship.

If only for humanitarian reasons we must assume a steady growth in energy consumption by the population increase of the world. Therefore, let us assume that in fifty years world-wide per capita consumption will reach that of present-day Sweden, which is two-thirds of the consumption per capita of the United States. Let us further assume that the world population, now 4 billion, will increase, as many experts in this field project, to 6 billion by the year 2000 and to 9 billion by 2025 with most of the increase occuring in the developing countries.

Under these circumstances, world-wide energy consumption in terms of oil equivalent would rise from about 6 billion tons in 1975 to 16 billion by the 2000 and close to 50 billion in 2025. This would represent an eight-fold increase in fifty years, implying an average annual increase in energy consumption of slightly more than 4 percent.

Let us now look at the known global energy resources presently and readily available. These include the principal sources of energy: namely, oil and gas, coal, and nuclear fission. I shall leave aside for the time being such renewable resources as solar and others which are practically unlimited but which at present are unharnessed, such as nuclear fusion. The figures I will give are, again, in terms of billions of tons of oil equivalent.

It is estimated that known reserves of oil and natural gas represent 200 to 600 billion tons and that coal reserves amount to between 3000 and 6000 billion tons. If the 4.2 percent growth rate I have mentioned were to prevail in the future, and oil should retain its present 50 percent share of total energy, oil would be exhausted within thirty to fifty years and coal by the end of the next century. On the other hand, proven uranium reserves, if used in nuclear power reactors commercially available today, would be equivalent to about 40 to 50 billion tons of oil: that is, one-fifth to one-quarter of the lower estimate of oil and gas resources. However, if these reserves were used in breeder reactors, the energy available from uranium would be multiplied by a factor of 100 to 1000, as a result of more efficient utilization of uranium and of the economic possibility of resorting to much poorer grade ores. A multiplication factor of 100 would bring obtainable energy to the level of that derivable from coal, while a 1000 factor would yield ten times as much energy as may be derivable from coal. This would mean an enormous quantitative change in available energy supply.

There are, of course, other energy sources available, such as hydro-power and geothermal. These sources, however, are relatively limited. It is practically a fact that the industrial world is fully utilizing available hydro-power under its jurisdiction; and while untapped sources such as that of the Amazon, the Congo, and other tropical rivers are considerable, it does not seem that these will have much impact on the global energy balance. More likely, hydroelectric power will not increase its present 5 to 6 percent share of world energy production. Similarly, geothermal springs and hot rocks, as energy sources, obviously make a local impact, but the contribution from these sources to global needs would have to be considered marginal.

From the viewpoint of decision-making let us now look at the energy source options or alternatives that are or will likely be available in the short and long-term. By short-term I mean a period of about twenty-five years. I pick this span of time because it approaches the time that it takes for a new technology to make a substantial contribution in the market for which it was designed. For instance, nuclear power is only now, some thirty-five years after its feasibility was demonstrated in the Chicago football stadium, beginning—after investment of tens of billions of dollars—to account for close to 10 percent of electricity production in the industrial countries. It will certainly take some twenty-five years more of steady construction of nuclear power plants before it reaches the 50 percent level. We must assume, therefore, that even with intensive research and development of the magnitude that has been applied to nuclear power, it will take decades before other options such as various forms of solar-related energy (solar, wind, tidal, ocean gradient, wave, etc.) could make a substantial impact on the energy economy of the world.

This means that for the next twenty-five years the principal options open to us are essentially four: namely, oil and gas, coal, nuclear, and conservation (chiefly in the more affluent industrial countries). Of course, other sources of energy, however limited, can and should be used. Small systems such as mini-water turbines, small-scale utilization of solar-derived energy, biomass and units of that type to meet the requirements of the villages in developing countries can be locally significant. But these small systems cannot provide the basis for industrialization and for major improvements in the standard of living, which the developing countries regard as their prerogative. I repeat: they regard it as their prerogative.

With regard to conservation, it is true that substantial amounts of energy can be saved in industrialized countries, but these measures, even if applied efficiently, will only temporarily change the slope of the growth curve. To the changing world belongs the continuous substitution of one technology for another, from the coal-burning steam engine, to the gasoline-combustion engine, to the electric motor.

And so it is only for the longer term, by the second and third decades of the next century, that it seems reasonable to expect that solar energy, in its various forms, and possibly nuclear fusion, will begin to play an important role—this, of course, provided that an intensive program of research and development is adopted. Both solar and nuclear fusion are potentially capable of affording an abundant source of power, once man learns to harness them.

The next question I proposed to discuss was what are the pros and cons of the principal options before us.

Petroleum is ideally suited as a source of fuel for transport by land, sea, and air and will be very hard to replace. The automobile industry has made, I believe, an enormous contribution to the freedom of movement of the individual, to the equalizing and perhaps to the democratization of society. It is a major element in industrial prosperity for most western countries and is becoming increasingly so in the socialist countries. I say this despite certain drawbacks of which we have become aware in the last two decades, as it is inconceivable today to imagine a world without the motor car. Strong arguments could then be made for confining the use of petroleum products almost exclusively to transport, not to mention the numerous chemical derivations of petroleum, and thereby stretch out our reserves until we are assured of the availability of other forms of auto-motive power, the electric car, hydrogen systems, or whatever the future may bring. I need not elaborate on the environmental effects of the petro-leum industry, as everyone is aware of these. (I would far rather live right next door to a nuclear reprocessing plant than to an oil refinery.)

When we examine coal, the main limiting factors are the social diffi-culties and environmental disadvantages of mining large quantities of coal, as well as the related infrastructure needed for its transport. If we install expensive equipment, we can reduce to an acceptable amount the emission of oxides of nitrogen, carbon monoxide, sulphur dioxide, hydrocarbon constituents, ash and other particulates. Other limits to the use of coal, and, indeed, of fossil fuels generally, may lie in the consequences of in-creased carbon dioxide concentration in the atmosphere. While scientists are not in agreement about the magnitude or form of such carbon dioxide effects, the expansion of fossil fuel consumption at the current rate of 4 percent a year will double the amount of carbon dioxide in the atmo-sphere by the middle of the next century, thus increasing the risk of serious climatic changes.

It should be noted here that another consideration in opting for a par-ticular source of energy is its geographical location. We are all aware that nature has been highly selective in distributing the world's oil reserves and the same, as a matter of fact, is true also of coal. Seventy percent of the world's oil reserves are in the Middle East, and 80 percent of the world's coal reserves are in three countries: the United States, the Soviet Union, and the People's Republic of China. One of the effects of the oil crisis of

1973 has been to stimulate countries to diversify as much as possible their energy supplies and to eliminate undue dependence on a particular source or a particular area. Even Iran has embarked on a large nuclear power program so as to diversify its energy base.

What I have said is also indicative of the fact, and, indeed, a reminder, that fossil fuels are finite. Perhaps, we should begin to realize that we have reached the beginning of the end of the fossil fuel age. Historically, we have used and consumed one fossil fuel reserve after the other—wood, coal, oil, and gas—each having had its turn as a major energy source. May I just remind you that in 1876 the energy need in the United States was met to 75 percent by burning wood; in 1925, 75 percent was provided by coal, and in 1975, again 75 percent was covered by oil. The geological processes through which coal and oil were formed took hundreds of millions of years. Should we continue to simply burn these resources when we know that they are indispensible for many other products deemed necessary by society? Or should we simply go on and risk the very likelihood of leaving future generations destitute of fossil fuels?

This brings me to another alternative, that of nuclear energy. Until the turn of the century, the predominant nuclear power plant will probably be the thermal fission reaction of the light water and Candu types. Nuclear power as developed now is best suited for the steady generation of large amounts of electrical energy from very large units. This is partly due to the relatively high initial capital investment but low fuel cost, and partly to economics of scale. Such power may be developed as a source of high-temperature heat for industrial processes, low-temperature heat for domestic use, and for large-scale ocean transport. The need for large nuclear power units limits its use in most developing countries where demand for electricity is still small. It also excludes the use of nuclear energy as a means of transport, except possibly, as I mentioned, by sea. Thus, broadly speaking, nuclear energy for the next several decades will be chiefly a source of electric power and its value to society will depend on its share of electric power in total energy use, a share that has been steadily rising.

I believe that today many of the fears about the safety of individual nuclear power stations have subsided. During twenty years of experience with civilian nuclear power plants, there has been not a single fatal accident caused by the nuclear part of the power plant or any unforeseen escape of radioactivity. This record, together with the numerous and extremely thorough studies that have been made on the matter have set the fears, at least on the informed public, at rest. As a result of Professor

Rasmussen's report, and other competent studies, concern today seems to have shifted from that of nuclear safety to that of long-term social implications. In other words, can society safely store nuclear wastes for long periods, maybe thousands of years? Will nuclear power lead inevitably to nuclear weapons proliferation? Must our attempts to avoid sabotage in hijacking lead to an authoritarian state?

We must recognize that each energy technology has its environmental and social price, and we must try dispassionately to compare these costs with the benefits conferred. The hazards created by several hundred tons of sulphur oxides and ashes emitted daily by large coal- and oil-burning plants and the steady increase in carbon dioxide in the atmosphere must be weighed against nuclear power risks. But it is essential to see these risks in their true perspective and to avoid the passion and near hysteria that today so often animates much of the debate.

The measures needed to ensure the security of nuclear installations will affect the individual society's freedom of movement much less than the controls we have already accepted for civilian air travel. If some countries can live with thousands of mobile nuclear explosives in the form of weapons—without establishing a police state—we surely shall not need such a state to deal with the security problems of the infinitely safer and far fewer nuclear power plants and related facilities.

Resolving the long-term storage or disposition of nuclear waste is the objective of promising research and development activity. There appears to be a consensus that high-level radioactive waste can be safely stored in geological structures, such as rock-salt and granite formations that have indications of stability over geological periods of time. However such storage has not yet been undertaken or even demonstrated. In the meantime the nuclear industry is using surface storage tanks and preparing to vitrify the high-level, liquid waste for an eventual, permanent disposal scheme which retains the possibility of retrieval. As I have implied, the particulate and noxious gaseous by-products from burning fossil fuels can be taken care of, but it is hardly feasible to remove the carbon-dioxide from the stack gases. Both carbon dioxide and nuclear wastes undoubtedly will be around for future generations—the first steadily building up in the atmosphere and the second probably being safely stored deep underground.

In this connection, it is interesting to recall that in the known case of a natural fission reaction which occurred nearly two billion years ago in Oklo, in Gabon, west Africa, the fission products that arose did not migrate significantly from the point at which the reaction took place, even though control over these was experienced only by nature. In the short term, therefore, decisions that must now be taken really concern the particular mix that a country will choose between energy conservation, fossil fuel, and nuclear power using thermal reactors. The answer will vary from country to country.

I have left until last the question of the risks of proliferation of nuclear weapons since it is a matter to which I would like to give particular attention in view of the responsibilities of the International Atomic Energy Agency.

I do not believe that the spread of nuclear weapons capacity is inescapably tied to the spread of nuclear power plants. The rapid growth and diffusion of scientific and technical knowledge has given a score of countries, besides the nuclear-weapons states, the possibility of exploiting nuclear energy for peaceful or for military purposes. The list of countries technologically able to make nuclear explosives is bound to grow, whatever we do about nuclear power. Moreover, a country wishing to produce fissile material or a weapon can do so far more easily by using a research reactor and a pilot reprocessing plant than by using the far more costly and complicated piece of equipment represented by a nuclear power station or commercial reprocessing plant.

This notwithstanding, the fear of seeing the spread of nuclear explosive technology should not lead to limitations of technological progress or to attempts to gain commercial advantage over nonnuclear-weapon countries. At the same time, however, all precautions should be taken to ensure that materials and installations provided for peaceful applications are not diverted to military purposes. It is toward this objective that the safeguards of the International Atomic Energy Agency have been developed.

The agency's system of inspection and verification now covers all nuclear power stations in the nonnuclear-weapon states. The system operates either under the safeguards system provided for by the Agency's statute, which has been operational since the early 1960s, or under the Non-Proliferation Treaty (NPT), which came into force in 1970. The earlier safeguards system covers specific installations, material, and transfers of technology. These safeguards are being applied, for example, to the facilities provided to Brazil by the Federal Republic of Germany. Since the advent of the NPT, the 98 nonnuclear-weapon states party to it, such as the Federal Republic of Germany, have accepted IAEA safeguards on *all* nuclear activities on their territories. France, one of the five nuclear-weapons states, has not signed the NPT but has repeatedly stated that it will behave as if it had signed the treaty with regard to deliveries of equipment to other countries.

Thus, for the first time in the history of mankind an international inspection system has been accepted. Since its operation a wealth of experience has been accumulated; and, even though there is always room for improvement, the system works well. In the future it may serve as a model for other similar undertakings in the realm of disarmament. While these safeguards cannot *prevent* a state from developing weapons, their *deterrence* value lies *first* in the international undertaking by the state not to use nuclear material for production of explosives or for anything but peaceful purposes, and *second* in the potential for timely detection of diversion of significant quantities of nuclear material.

What is the responsibility of decision-makers with regard to the prevention of proliferation of nuclear weapons? For an important nuclear materials exporter like the United States, it lies in assuring that any exported material or equipment comes under IAEA safeguards, preferably through the application of the Non-Proliferation Treaty which requires safeguards on *all* peaceful nuclear activities of the importing state. Those states which import nuclear plant and equipment must set up a national system for accounting and control of nuclear materials which is in turn verified by the IAEA. The importance of making this system universal in nonnuclear-weapons states, that is, covering all nuclear materials in all activities, is not just to make the checking up easier but also to create an atmosphere of mutual confidence in which the commerce in nuclear materials can flow unimpeded, as well as the exchange of scientific and technical information.

The nonnuclear-weapon states which joined the Non-Proliferation Treaty did so with the understanding that once the horizontal proliferation of nuclear weapons had been checked, the nuclear-weapon powers would do something about their vertical proliferation; a *complete test ban* would be a positive first step, but it has so far eluded us. Another important encouragement for states to join the nonproliferation regime would be an increase in assistance and exchange of information, putting them in an advantageous position vis-à-vis those still outside the treaty. So far, this has not been the case, but some donor countries have started to limit their technical assistance only to countries that have accepted the NPT.

I have attempted to demonstrate that, in the short-term, the critical decisions that must be taken now really concern the particular mix that a country will choose between energy conservation, fossil fuels, and nuclear power using thermal reactors. The answer will vary from country to country. Whatever choices the Western market economics make, it is clear that centralized economy countries and many developing countries will forge ahead with nuclear power.

As for the *longer* term—decisions that will have to be taken around the turn of this century—as can be expected, the horizon is far less clear. We have no idea at this stage whether fusion energy will even be in sight. We also have little indication whether the *direct conversion* of solar energy into electricity and efficient energy storage systems that would be needed for the use of solar energy will be commercially available. The only additional options of which we have some assurances at this stage are the use of solar energy for domestic heat and the fast breeder reactor.

It seems to me reasonable that any decision-maker will ensure that his range of choices, now and in twenty-five years' time, is as wide as possible and that he will not deliberately eliminate a particular option unless it is demonstrably unacceptable. The so-called plutonium economy which the fast breeder reactor would involve would certainly entail problems which should be carefully studied and solutions sought. The risks of proliferation and of sabotage may or may not be greater than those associated with the current generation of reactors. One thing, however, is clear: The development of the fast breeder will provide an almost unlimited source of energy and will *avoid* the risk of competition for the world's uranium resources between the industrialized countries, which would be the first to use breeders on a large scale, and the developing countries. If we do not introduce fast breeders, the era of nuclear power from fission may not long survive the era of oil and natural gas. Our choices will be greatly narrowed, to the detriment of the well-being and progress of society.

We are all aware that we are living in a changing world, if only because of the constant reminder of a rapidly increasing world population: 4 billion people now and more than 6 billion by the turn of the century. If political stability throughout the world is to be maintained, these billions have to be fed. This will require the mobilization of all available human ingenuity. Just to meet such an enormously increased demand for food it would seem that greatly intensified agricultural methods need to be applied. This, of course, would mean more and more energy.

Under these circumstances I don't think that we are in a position to speak about a choice between different alternatives that may supply us with energy. I think we must use all of them in appropriate places and at the appropriate time, bearing in mind the finite nature of fossil fuels. But we must also be ready to accept new technologies. A tremendous amount of research has gone into the development of nuclear energy, and I don't see how mankind could satisfy its ever increasing energy needs without using this new energy source. This does not mean that all problems have been solved with nuclear energy in spite of its present high standard, but there is a continuous striving toward improvements based on acquired experience, improvements pursued more intensely than in any other energy-producing industry.

I would like to note some of the decisions that should be taken now.

One such decision should concern the impact on the environment of different energy-producing systems. Much has been done but, as yet, we have only scratched the surface. A fundamental problem here is the pollution of the atmosphere caused by combustion: Will it lead to an increase or decrease in the surface temperature of the earth?

Another important decision concerns support for research and development on solar energy: for both small, cheap units pumping water or heating water and larger systems in the megawatt bracket producing electricity.

There should also be a decision taken to study as thoroughly as possible the economic and other consequences of reprocessing spent fuel from present thermal reactors and recycling the plutonium: first, in thermal systems, later in breeder systems. An international undertaking should be started for reprocessing, waste disposal, and fuel manufacturing.

The development of a full-scale breeder reactor should be the object of close international collaboration. This would enhance the efficiency of the various resources and facilities now being used in a number of countries. Also studies should be undertaken for the use of power breeders for the production of process heat and desalting of water.

The international safeguarding system should be further developed to ascertain that an increased use of nuclear power does not lead to unauthorized use of nuclear explosives. Please be aware that the nuclear threat from nuclear weapons will continue to be with mankind even if nuclear power is eliminated as an energy alternative.

Being a layman with regard to space matters, I may be even more impressed by what has been achieved there than in the field of nuclear energy, in both cases through the ingenuity of men and by a systematic and concentrated application of science and technology. Man's curiosity and his efforts to find the truth and to apply his findings for the betterment of the life of his fellow beings cannot be stopped by artificial means and that is the fundamental reason why I do not think it is possible to put the lid over future application of nuclear energy for power generation. We may be wrong in our estimates of how much and when but an alternative to the classical energy sources has been invented and will certainly be used.

I believe that nuclear energy is essential and that it can and will play a leading role in providing a solution to the increasing demands of energy, mostly in the form of electricity, throughout the world. Its proper utilization will bring changes that will help transform the world to the benefit of mankind.

6

The New International Economic Order: Aspirations and Realities

Roberto de Oliveira Campos

The Great Confrontations

The changing international landscape of the post-war period is marked by three great confrontations, which to a certain extent overlap each other: the *ideological* confrontation of the Cold War, the *political* confrontation of decolonization, and the *economic* confrontation involved in the so-called North-South dialogue. I prefer to call the last one the "TNT confrontation" between tropical and temperate zones, for the simple reason that some of the most populous underdeveloped areas—India, Pakistan, Bangladesh, Egypt—lie in the northern hemisphere, while Australia, New Zealand, South Africa (and perhaps Argentina) can be regarded as developed countries in the southern hemisphere.

Now the *ideological* confrontation may be with us for some time to come, despite the efforts at détente. This is largely because of two factors. First, differences in motivation between the East and West. Second, a certain degree of asymmetry of behavior since the West preaches ideological pluralism and the East practices ideological rigidity. The East expects the West to countenance ideological erosion of its values, but is not apt to accept the besmirching of socialist purity by electoral democracy. But despite this asymmetry of behavior, the ideological confrontation has lost much of its sting and has ceased to be as obsessive a preoccupation as it was in the Cold War days.

The second confrontation, now coming to an end, was the *political* confrontation that led to the dissolution of Western colonial empires in the post-war period. Decolonization proceeded rather fast. The Algerian liberation war, the first phase of the Vietnam conflict until Diem Bien Phu, and the bloody skirmishes that preceded the Portuguese withdrawal from Africa were perhaps the last true colonial wars. They were replaced

by even bloodier tribal strife and ideological rivalries, such as happened
in Nigeria, the former Belgian Congo, and Angola. A potential conflict
lurks ominously in the southern part of the African continent, mixing
three ingredients: tribal and racial clash and ideological strife.

In Asia, the conflicts have always been much more ideological in motivation: to wit, Vietnam, Laos, and Cambodia. As conflicts in the Third
World—a convenient appellation which is increasingly unhelpful to describe the complexity of the developing world—as conflicts in the Third
World become more internalized, and gradual accommodation is reached
with the postimperial West, the political solidarity between the several
components of the underdeveloped world begins to waver. The con-
ferences of Bandung in 1955, led by Nehru and Sukarno, and of Belgrade
in 1961, led by Tito and Nasser, marked perhaps the high mark of political
coalescence of developing countries in response to the paramount confrontation of the anticolonial and Cold War struggles.

The third attempt at forming a coalition of the underdeveloped world
(encompassing this time Latin America which was hardly a voice in
Bandung and Belgrade) is reflected in the claims for a new international
economic order, which is a response to the *economic* confrontation between the rich and the poor world of nations. But more of this later.

The Balance-of-Power Scenario

Clearly intertwined with the phases of confrontation is the question of
the organization of power relationships. These may be said to have
evolved from a short-lived American nuclear monopoly in the immediate postwar period to strategic bipolarity in the 1950s and gradually,
during the 1960s, to a "balance-of-power scenario." The latter is slowly
yielding to pressures for recognition of a broader interdependence. In
both the political and the economic field there has been a perceptible
movement from duopoly to pentarchy, and then to polyarchy and multi-
polarity.

The solitary confrontation of the two superpowers, the United States
and Russia, in the 1950s—the only powers that possess overkill capability
—has already given way to a "balance-of-power" scenario. In the socialist
camp this evolution away from solitary confrontation was due not only
to the Chinese heresy but also to rising forces of nationalism that are
eroding ideological orthodoxy. This is evidenced by the emergence of
several varieties of national communism as well as by the rise of Euro-
communism, an uncertain and probably unstable betrothal between Com-

munism and democracy. The Western camp, on the other hand, never presented a conformist and monolithic picture. While some earlier challenges, such as the Gaullist nationalism in France, have abated, the real or perceived erosion of the power of the United States, and above all its fatigue of leadership, as both a provider and a gendarme, have facilitated the revival of the balance-of-power approach to international politics. There are those who think in terms of a three-and-a-half world, in which political responsibility as well as economic and military power would be basically shared by the United States, Soviet Russia, and the European Economic Community, with Japan holding an intermediate position as an economic giant but a political and military pygmy. Others visualize a balance-of-power pentarchy, by the inclusion of Communist China as an emergent nuclear power capable, despite its economic weakness, of exercising considerable political clout in southeastern Asia and some ideological influence in other areas of the world, notably Africa.

The picture, however, is far from simple. And perhaps the attempt to resuscitate the balance-of-power system of the nineteenth century is based on the perception of false historical analogies. The great powers during the nineteenth century were balanced by the disposition of using force in the centers of power. This, however, is unthinkable in the nuclear age. Moreover, all of the actors then claimed a world rule. Today all but two of the actors can claim only a regional rule for they are no more than regional powers.

Finally, the pentarchical balance of power conceptualization faces today very strong challenges. It is of course opposed by rising regional powers such as Brazil, Iran, India, Australia, and, perhaps, Nigeria, which in their own scenarios have a combination of ingredients causing them to want a meaningful role in international decisions. They all want a polyarchy rather than a pentarchy.

A second challenge comes from the major redistribution of financial power and liquidity brought about by the OPEC cartel, which also exposed the vulnerability of industrialized economies to supply restrictions by disciplined producers' cartels. Some Third World countries became price-makers rather than price-takers in the world arena.

The third element in the increasing assertiveness of developing countries, claims for a more genuinely multilateral mechanism of decision-making and for the establishment of a new international economic order, derives from the fact that they regard the concepts of duopoly and balance of power as outmoded models and press hard for the implantation of a genuinely multilateral diplomacy. From Bandung and Belgrade, which

were largely statements of political principles, they moved to concrete
economic issues, first in the Algiers conference, which created the so-
called group of 77, and then in four successive meetings of the United
Nations Conference on Trade and Development. In this sense it might be
said that OPEC and UNCTAD are the trade unions of the underdeveloped
world trying to increase its collective bargaining power vis-à-vis the industrialized nations.

Changing Power Relationships

This new militancy of developing countries in the international arena has
been prompted by a number of real or perceived changes in power relationships. First, the decline in what might be called the "positive" power
of the superpowers. The nuclear impasse limited their intervention capability and eroded the traditional linkage between *power* and *order.* Con-
sequently, it enabled the smaller countries to use their "negative" power
of challenging the existing economic order and prevailing international
institutional arrangements. Second, as the oil crisis created a new awareness of supply limitations of basic ingredients of growth for the industrialized world, there grew in raw material exporting countries of the
Third World a probably exaggerated perception of the finiteness of resources. Third, there was a realization that important socioeconomic
changes, such as decolonization and expropriation or nationalization of
mines and properties, had shrunk the manipulative power over raw material supplies, previously enjoyed by industrialized countries. The fourth
element was the discovery of a possible "trade union effect" in international trade through the adoption by producers of collective bargaining
procedures in the form of cartels or of producer marketing associations.
    A rather interesting additional factor is the relative depoliticization of
relations within the industrialized world, since the gospel of a "new international economic order" is preached by countries of diverse ideological trends and diverse political institutions. The difference between the
moderates and the revolutionaries lies more in the stridency of the tone
than in the substance of the doctrine.
    As the struggle of developing countries for striking a better deal with the
industrial countries proceeds in several international fora, it is important
to separate confused hopes from practical objectives, ideological precon-
ceptions from objective analysis. Some of the grievances are well founded.
Indeed, existing organizations of economic cooperation appear to have
been structured in a direction favorable to the interest of industrialized

countries. The General Agreement of Tariffs and Trade, for instance, has in practice been successful only in reducing tariff barriers; this has been very helpful to the trade in manufactures, while leaving relatively untouched nontariff barriers. Those take the form of quotas, quantitative restrictions, and internal production subsidies, which are particularly harmful to export of agricultural and livestock products, as well as to labor-intensive manufactures originating in developing countries.

In the financial sphere, when the "Special Drawing Rights" were created by the International Monetary Fund, 70 percent of the new liquidity was assigned to assist major trading countries; no agreement has been reached so far on the use of this facility for financing economic development. The export drive of industrialized countries is usually regarded as a display of competitiveness and efficiency, while similar efforts of developing countries are rather quaintly described as "market disruption."

In the throes of the present recession the industrialized countries have resorted more and more to what Professor Ralph Dahrendorf calls the "Thalidomide of Protectionism" by attempting to reduce their unemployment by exporting it to the poorer countries. Commodity agreements aimed at stabilizing prices or incomes of primary producers have been accepted only reluctantly. The industrialized countries appear to show more interest in the "guarantee-of-supply" features to reassure the consumers than in the "guarantee-of-income" aspect to benefit the producers. No wonder then that primary producers turn often to naive capitalization efforts in order to improve their bargaining power. No wonder also that, although some of them (precisely the poorest ones) have been grievously hurt by the rising oil prices, most developing countries entertain a grudging admiration for the ability of the OPEC countries to challange the established order, thus moving from a passive price-taking role to an active price-making position in world trade.

Assessing Bargaining Power

In assessing the bargaining power of developing countries some caveats are in order. The first limitation lies precisely in the enormous diversity of developing countries in terms of resources as well as actual and potential economic capabilities, a diversity that can no longer be meaningfully covered by the wornout expression "Third World." The expression "Third World" is traced by some to Alfred Sauvy and by others to Frantz Fanon, who wrote *The Wretched of the Earth* and coined the marvelous phrase that "revolution is the carnival of the oppressed." The appellation "Third World" should perhaps be reserved to the OPEC group and to some semiindustrialized countries with considerable export potential such as Brazil, Mexico, and Colombia. But we also have to distinguish a "Fourth World," embodying some populous countries with an unfavorable man-resource ratio and still rather low per capita income such as India and Pakistan. There also is a "Fifth World" formed by really disadvantaged countries, such as Bangladesh or the Sahel countries in Central Africa, poorly endowed with natural resources and condemned for a long time to remain below the poverty line.

A second caveat has to deal with the frequent overestimation of the manipulative price-making capability typified by the oil cartel. But oil is a very special commodity and other producers' attempts at cartelization have been much less successful. Phosphate producers benefited from sharp but short-lived price rises. Bauxite producers were only moderately successful in improving their earnings, while the copper cartel failed to arrest the price decline resulting from the world recession. It also must be borne in mind that some developed industrialized countries—the United States, Canada, Australia, the Soviet Union—are major producers and exporters of primary commodities such as iron ore, copper, nickel, zinc, bauxite, cotton, and sugar, while some developing countries are vitally dependent on imports thereof. In fact, 55 percent, no less, of world commodity exports come from industrialized countries and not from primary producers. Moreover, the possibilities of technological substitution enhance the capability of industrialized countries to resist upward price pressures. A new deal for raw material producers is therefore unlikely to be brought about only by pressures from primary producers. It will require acceptance in industrialized countries of the view that their best interest lies in a better distribution of world income.

This is not to deny that there are important socioeconomic transformations which have occurred and which strengthened the hand of developing countries in the international arena. This new strength does not come from an apocalyptic forecast of a physical scarcity of raw materials, as visualized by the Club of Rome. For a combination of new technologies, recycling and price-induced new research and exploitation may delay the onset of the age of scarcity. But there are socioeconomic factors, perhaps more important and often overlooked in current discussions, that will improve the manipulative position of developing countries. The traditional consumer ownership of supply sources is being torn asunder by nationalist and socialist trends in producing countries, leading to outright takeovers of foreign properties or to increased pressures to retain at home a larger share of income via wages or local taxes. Transfer-pricing, made possible hitherto by the integrated operation of multinational companies that, at times, choose to realize profits abroad rather than at the raw material exporting stage, is frowned upon and likely to be henceforth severely restrained.

The present accumulation of foreign indebtedness by developing countries, in addition to nationalist pressures, tends to discourage new investments, particularly in the fields of capital-intensive mineral exploitation. And while there is substantial room for upgrading agricultural productivity in the developing countries, producers' cartels or market coordination efforts will undoubtedly be made to retain for the producers a larger share of productivity increases which formerly benefited consumers in industrialized countries.

Finally, supply disruptions in both mining and agriculture may recur periodically in politically unstable areas such as Africa and the Middle East where religious, racial, or tribal conflicts are far from extinguished.

On Allocating the Guilt

It is now time for an essay on the allocation of guilt as between the actors in the confrontation play of the new international economic order: the industrialized countries on the one hand and the developing countries on the other. It cannot be gainsaid that industrialized countries have indulged in institutionalized hypocrisy in their relations with the poorer developing countries. This institutionalized hypocrisy takes various forms. First, paying lip-service to liberal trade policies and yet adopting protectionist measures precisely where they hurt more—that is, in relation to agricultural products and simple manufactured goods— thus shrinking the only market opportunities open to low-technology developing countries. Second, singing praise to free-market forces when facing pressures of developing countries for commodity agreements or buffer stocks, and yet dropping any pretense of belief in the divinity of the market when dealing internally with farmers or with inefficient manufacturing sectors. This is a rather peculiar pattern of behavior. The Brazilians after the frost of 1975 found that the international community viewed the rise in coffee prices due to exhaustion of stocks and physical reduction of supplies as not so much an "act of God" but as some sort of obscene speculative manipulation. However, when later the prices of citrus fruits and tomatoes rose in Florida, due also to a frost, the Americans immediately rediscovered the divinity of the laws of the market.

A third form of hypocrisy involves giving theoretical recognition to political and economic interdependence and yet refusing to share meaningful decision-making, which continues to be done through a directorate of major powers rather than through general multilateral consultation, notably in matters concerned with the international monetary system. The "Trilateral Commission," which appears to have a discreet but perceptible and probably powerful influence on current foreign trade policies of the United States, epitomizes this approach.

A peculiar behavior is what I call the "blinker effect," or the microsectorial approach. This consists in taking protectionist decisions on the basis of the impact of unemployment on particular industries or sectors, while forgetting the global employment effects derived from the overall balance of trade. Thus, the United States imposed taxes on Brazilian footwear and demanded the establishment of "voluntary" quotas on textiles in 1975, a year in which it achieved a trade surplus with Brazil of no less than 1.4 billion dollars, or about seven times the value of Brazil's "offending" exports. Clearly, the employment-destroying effect of Brazilian exports of the so-called sensitive goods was far lower than the employment-creating effect for American industries benefiting from the huge export surplus.

To prove that they also can be illogical, the West Germans maintained restrictions on our textile goods even after we demonstrated to them that the value of our imports of German textile machinery and equipment was much higher and therefore represented net employment creation in a high technology sector.

It is surely high time that measures to defend employment in industrialized countries be taken in the light of the total employment effects of the trade of the offending country rather than under the pressure of narrow sectoral interests. A developing country that has a net overall trade deficit with an industrialized country is creating and not destroying employment there, and should be accordingly treated. This, despite the inconvenience caused to individual sectors in the industrialized country that could or should be helped through adjustment assistance and not through protectionist measures.

This brings me to two observations that might prove rather controversial. The first is that the conventional concept of "dumping" deserves redefinition. When the offending country practices dumping, that is, sells abroad

at prices lower than domestic price minus value-added taxes, and still
suffers a trade deficit in relation to the aggrieved country, it is in reality
subsidizing the foreign consumer and not destroying net employment.
The rage and fury against low-price manufactures of developing countries
allegedly dumped in industrialized markets should be reserved for cases
in which the offending country has an equilibrium or surplus trade position with the importing country. Only then would it be unfairly robbing
unemployment.

My second observation is to utter a word of praise for the Japanese
whose trade policies are now rather unpopular in other OECD countries
in Europe because of their large trade surplus vis-à-vis both the United
States and the European Economic Community. From the viewpoint of
developing countries, the industrial policies of Japan have been rather
constructive. Not being able to import labor into their crowded island,
they exported factories and relinquished to cheaper labor countries—
Korea, Formosa, Singapore, and now Brazil—labor-intensive industries
such as textiles and electronics components, while concentrating on
high-technology fields and heavy mechanical goods. European countries,
notably Germany and Switzerland, imported labor when they might
have exported factories. The United States, through its multinational
companies, did export both capital and factories but, by subsidizing or
protecting low-technology industries that lost their comparative advantage, refused in fact to undertake the necessary internal structural
adjustments.

Demonology and Escapism in Developing Countries

This exercise in allocation of guilt would be incomplete and unfair if I
were not to allocate blame also to developing countries for their propensity for *escapism* and *demonology.*

Both are very often present in the inflamed rhetoric of the advocates
of the new international economic order. The escapist bent consists of
externalizing the guilt by continuously faulting imperialist domination
for domestic inequities, while forgetting the need for internal reform,
notably in agricultural policies, land tenure, fiscal practices, and population planning. This escapist syndrome is at the root of the now-popular
dependency theory, for which I have little use or patience. This doctrine, invented in Latin America and subsequently exported to other
areas, attributes distorted consumption patterns and alienated class at-

titudes to the influence of international capitalism. This theory appears to relegate policy makers and administrators within developing countries to the humiliating positions of puppets or idiots.

It must also be recognized that developing countries fail, not infrequently, to take advantage of trade opportunities because of internal inflation and overvalued exchange rates. Misguided nationalism may also at times retard or impede the exploitation of natural resources for which there is a world demand. And finally, they often adopt industrialization policies biased against agriculture, thus converting themselves into inefficient industrial producers and net food importers.

The legitimate case and rational protest of developing countries against the established order are also infirmed by exercises in *demonology.* The new demons are the much-maligned multinational corporations. The surge of multinational corporations as an efficient form of economic organization capable of controlling a substantial share of the world production and trade is not, of course, a new phenomenon. Only recently however it began to be dramatized, largely because of the alleged capacity of the multinationals, grossly overrated in my view, for political manipulation in host countries. They are accused of deciding on levels of production and export as a function of their global strategy rather than of host country national interest. Or of deforming native consumption habits in the direction of wasteful consumption patterns of wealthy societies. Or of minimizing the fiscal burden by convenient manipulation of trading prices between subsidiaries in different countries. Or of asphyxiating weak national competitors in order to gain monopoly power. While there is a pittance of truth in all those strictures, the fact remains that multinationals are the best instrument so far devised to achieve the transfer of technology, to tap international capital markets, and to promote interregional trade. Given the panoply of powers at the disposal of governments, it is not beyond the capability of even the weakest of the developing countries to cause multinationals, by negotiation, persuasion or compulsion, to reconcile their global strategy with rationally defined national interests. The recipe for developing countries is surely not to shut themselves off from the technological, financial, and trading contribution of multinational companies but, rather, first, to diversify their origin so as to promote competition rather than collusion and, second, to strengthen the national entrepreneur by financial and technical assistance and a judicious application of antitrust laws. I cannot escape the impression that the level of prepotency of multinationals is a direct function of the degree of incompetence of governments.

While some of the claims of developing countries are unrealistic, and, at times, counterproductive, and their rhetoric unduly strident, there is an economic, political, and ethical dimension to the demands for a new international economic order that industrialized countries could only ignore at the cost of political polarization and disruptive economic action. We are witnessing a long-term movement and not a passing fad.

The most mature expression of the aspirations of developing nations was reached in the Nairobi conference called UNCTAD IV. Discussions took place under eight main headings: commodities, including the "integrated program" and the common fund for buffer stocks; expansion and diversification of exports of manufactures and semimanufactures from less developed countries; money and finance, including debt problems, balance-of-payment adjustments and reform of the international monetary system; the transfer of technology—that is, a code of conduct for multinational corporations—and the impact of the patent system on the less developed countries; special measures for disadvantaged countries; economic cooperation between developing countries; trade with socialist countries; and institutional reform, including the strengthening of UNCTAD.

Commodities were the most important of the topics because 80 percent of the income of the less developed countries derives from only twelve commodities. Here the developing countries favored an integrated approach, which would include international buffer stocks, creation of a common fund for financing of stocks, improved compensatory financing for losses in export revenues, a system of multinational commitments and long-term contracts for individual commodities, and expansion of processing activities in developing countries. Seventeen products were selected as particularly relevant for the less developed countries, and ten of them—cocoa, coffee, copper, cotton, jute, rubber, sisal, sugar, tea, and tin—were described as "core" commodities for buffer stock schemes.

The attitude of the industrialized countries was, in general, dilatory and hostile to the proposals for an integrated treatment of commodity problems via a common fund, preference being expressed for a "case-by-case" approach. Among the industrialized nations, the Scandinavian countries and the European Economic Community, with the possible exception of West Germany, have generally shown a more flexible and accommodating attitude than the United States, West Germany, and Japan.

The European Economic Community had, of course, already agreed to a modest income stabilization mechanism by signing in 1974 the Lomé Convention, which benefited forty-nine countries in the Caribbean, African and Pacific areas. More recently, the European Economic Community has agreed to the principle of, but not the operational mechanism for, a common fund to finance the stockpiling of commodities.

In relation to the Lomé Convention, the two main objections that can be offered are that, first, it creates a new discrimination within the developing world by ignoring Latin America and most countries in Asia. It is therefore conducive to greater discrimination rather than to an attenuation of discriminatory practices. The second objection is that the scope of the fund is much too modest to make a dent in the problem of commodity price and income stabilization.

On financial questions, the Nairobi conference concentrated on debt relief. The group of 77 had proposed cancellation of debts for the least developed countries, relief on bilateral debts of other developing countries, and rescheduling of commercial debts over twenty-five years through the creation of a refinancing agency. Again, the posture of the industrialized countries was to agree to the principle of relief but only on a case-by-case basis. No agreement was also reached on another old grievance of the less developed countries in several fora of the U.N., that is, their demand for linkage of the issuance of the Special Drawing Rights of the Monetary Fund to automatic development lending.

Options of Industrialized Countries

What are now the options for the industrialized countries in the face of mounting pressures from the developing countries for a new international economic order?

To use a felicitous expression of Guy F. Erb,[1] there are three options for the industrialized countries: confrontation, selection accommodation with newly powerful nations, or cooperation in a multilateral framework. The latter—*multilateral international cooperation*—is by far to be preferred, although the second, *selective accommodation,* may be more practical as an intermediate step.

In the economic field, the improvement of the trade positions of developing countries may require internal adjustments in the rich countries in order to lessen obstacles to trade and make room for the much needed diversification of exports of the developing world. In the political field, there need be greater acceptance by industrialized countries of diverse political systems, different ideological preferences and institutional arrangements that may not only be different from those of the Western world, but actually imply a criticism of its value system.

The Different Faces of Authoritarianism

By way of parenthesis it can be noted that current political trends are quite divergent as between the Western developed world and developing countries. The postwar period has witnessed the consolidation and the expansion of democratic institutions in the defeated powers—Western Germany, Italy, and Japan—and, more recently, in the peripheral areas of the Western European system—Greece, Spain, and Portugal. This has even contaminated the Communist parties which, with yet untested sincerity, appear willing to abandon their revolutionary stance in favor of the electoral way of capturing power.

By contrast, the vast majority of developing nations practice some form of authoritarianism. In fact, no more than a score of nations among the approximately 152 nations that compose the political universe can be said to practice democracy in the Western sense. Thus authoritarianism, far from being a case of political pathology, is probably the most prevalent form of political organization in the world.

This makes it important to distinguish several types of authoritarianism rather than clinging to the naive "black-and-white approach," *democracy* vs. *dictatorship*. In fact many of the authoritarian regimes within the Third World can be described as "authoriarian-liberal"—if you pardon the contradiction of words—as opposed to "authoritarian-totalist." Authoritarian-totalist regimes are, for instance, those of Communist countries and of some rather primitive dictatorships in Africa and Latin American. The authoritarian-liberal regimes, on the other hand, uphold democracy as a professed and accepted objective. They do not impose ideological conformity; they maintain, at least in a formal sense, democratic institutions; they admit of economic pluralism; and they preserve various degrees of personal freedom. In fact the task of humanizing authoritarianism may be more relevant for the majority of developing countries than importing Western patterns of democratic organization. The importation of those forms without adequate political education may accentuate regional and tribal centrifugal pressures and make it more difficult to restrain consumption and mobilize, compulsorily, investment resources.

"Concertation" or Confrontation?

Let us now resume, after this parenthesis, the core of our discussion. The costs of adjustment to a new international economic order (the costs of *concertation,* to use a French neologism) must be weighed against the costs of *confrontation*. Those may be significant indeed. For industrialized countries, as noted by Guy F. Erb, those costs may include higher prices for imported raw materials, proliferation and the intensification of investment disputes, recrudescence of internal protectionism to the detriment of consumers, declining foreign markets for exports due to reduced buying capacity of the developing countries, vulnerability to restrictive action by raw material producers, and, last but not least, increasing friction in areas where global cooperation is imperative, such as environmental protection, health measures, and control of the seas.

Despite their revolutionary rhetoric, developing countries must also recognize and assess objectively the heavy costs of confrontation. Those costs lie in a greater need for defensive commodity stockpiling; in the shrinkage of the area of cooperation within the United Nations institutions; in the hardening of trade policy vis-à-vis developing countries' exports of raw materials and processed commodities; in the intensification of protectionism in industrialized countries by means of countervailing duties and the so-called voluntary export restraint programs for *sensitive* products exported by developing countries; in a decline in bilateral assistance programs; in the reduced funding of international lending institutions; and finally, in the discouragement of private investment.

A Recipe for Mutual Understanding

What appears to be needed at this juncture is a genuine, as distinct from a rhetorical, acceptance of the concept of *interdependence*. After all, rich and poor nations are condemned to exist aboard the spaceship earth, and prosperity cannot coexist indefinitely with abysmal poverty. Developing countries in international fora must eschew the temptation of accusatory rhetoric—that is their usual penchant for *escapism* (omitting the importance of internal reforms) and *demonology* (attributing underdevelopment to external forces of evil).

The industrialized countries—some of which hold the cynical view that in terms of power politics the developing countries are a nuisance but not yet a danger—must in turn abandon their hypocritical stance of paying lip-service to multilateral decision-making while adhering strictly to a key-country directorate approach; of recognizing the developing countries need for a better deal on trade and yet clamping quotas on imports of "sensitive" goods and subsidizing agricultural products in direct competition with poorer countries that have much fewer alternatives of production.

If the successive meetings of UNCTAD are interpreted as meetings of the trade unions of the underdeveloped world trying to improve their collective bargaining power vis-à-vis the wealthier segment of the world society, and indulging occasionally (as trade unions do) in the fancy of threatening with the strike weapon, perhaps this process can be regarded as a slow and confusing but legitimate means of promoting solidarity through redistribution rather than revolution through confrontation.

Above all, to borrow an expression of Mahbub ul Haq, Director of Policy Planning and Program Review of the World Bank, it is time to achieve the philosophical breakthrough in which the world arrives at the point ". . . when the development of poor nations is considered an essential element for the sustained development of rich nations and when the interests of both rich and poor nations are regarded as complementary and compatible rather than conflicting and irreconcilable."[2]

May the day soon come to pass when we cross this philosophical bridge.

Notes

1. Guy F. Erb, The Development World's "Challenge" in Perspective, in *Beyond Planning,* Overseas Development Council, 1975, pp. 148–149.

2. Mahbub ul Haq, "Negotiating a New Bargain with the Rich Counties," in *Beyond Planning,* Overseas Development Council, 1975, p. 157.

7

Challenge of the Next Two Decades: Dangers and Opportunities

Georgi A. Arbatov

It has been proposed that the lecturers cast a glance twenty years ahead, from the viewpoint of changes worked by science and technology to the consequences of these changes for global security in the broadest sense of the term. With respect to the future development of science and technology, I do not have the special knowledge required for a competent estimate, so I will limit myself to the rather general statement that there is no reason to expect a decline in the rate of scientific and technical progress, in the rate of introduction of innovations. The rate will increase, rather, because most countries have focused their national policy on encouragement of such development.

It is indisputable that accelerated scientific and technological progress works changes and produces a profound influence on all aspects of human life. The anxiety expressed in the background paper prepared for this series is, beyond doubt, due to the fact that this influence has so far been of a very contradictory nature. It appears that the chief contradiction consists in the fact that an excessively large proportion of the scientific and technological resources and efforts have been concentrated on the arms race and not on constructive purposes. There are other obvious contradictions, too, connected with problems of resources, employment, environment, and so forth. However, I shall not deal with these matters.

I would like to draw attention to another striking contradiction: though the achievements of our technological civilization are tremendous, they have as yet affected many of the fundamental problems confronting humanity in a very small degree. These achievements have hardly benefited the majority of mankind; in many respects they have only accentuated the contrasts both between individual societies and within many of them.

It is a fact that we live in a world where space laboratories and jet liners fly over vast regions of the planet that are inhabited by hundreds of

millions of people doomed to suffer hunger and desperate need almost
like many centuries ago; in a world where computers and the most advanced technology still exist side by side with fascist dictatorships practicing medieval tortures in countries like Chile, South Korea, and Uruguay;
in a world where supreme scientific achievement, hundreds of advanced
research centers such as MIT, coexist with ignorance, intellectual darkness,
and illiteracy among millions of peoples.

Such contrasts and contradictions abound even in the United States. The
past twenty years have been a period of vigorous growth in America's
scientific, technological, and industrial potential. But this was also a period
of decline of many of America's huge cities, of raging crime and violence,
of mounting economic and social difficulties.

If we try to look into the future on the basis of experience accumulated
in the past decades, we shall, apparently, arrive at another valid conclusion: There is no reason to believe that the changes science and technology
work in society will automatically eliminate these contradictions and
acquire a purely positive character. On the contrary, we can say for sure
that, as in the past, we shall continue to witness development of an
extremely contradictory nature.

Of course, this does not stem from science and technology, as such, but
from far-from-perfect social and political conditions and institutions. In
the context of rapid scientific and technological progress this fact has
given rise to many dangers.

The most obvious of these is the threat of war. Though this threat dates
back to the earliest times, scientific and technological achievements have
given it a new dimension, turning it into an issue of survival of human
society. As far as the approach to its solution is concerned, it should be
stated that the past twenty years were a period of the most dangerous
mistakes and at the same time of some revelations, a period of mounting
threats and at the same time of first initiatives designed to forestall them.
The next twenty years will be fraught with particularly grave dangers and
at the same time will offer great opportunities. As I see it, the realization
of these opportunities is the most vital task confronting mankind. The fact
that science and technology are developing faster than many of the economic, social, and political institutions on the planet should not be regarded as evil. This is a component part of the dialectics of development
which ensures progress in this particular case, prescribing changes in these
institutions.

In this respect the past few decades have been significant, for, as we see
it, the development of science and technology brought about shifts in the

minds of millions of people, revealing the widening discrepancy between possibilities and reality, between the things modern civilization can give man and humanity and what it actually gives or rather does not give them. We do not have to have great imagination to forecast for the next twenty years mounting pressures to adapt existing sociopolitical realities to the present level of scientific and technological potentialities.

Permit me now to refer to the list of concrete problems given in the background paper. These problems, namely prevention of nuclear war, arms limitations, the gap between "rich" and "poor" nations, approaching shortages of many types of resources and food, danger of upsetting the ecological balance, and so forth, are being discussed with rising eagerness. This shows in itself that the recent period has been fruitful in the sense of our perception and comprehension of problems confronting mankind. This is perhaps one of the most outstanding achievements of the past twenty-year period. We have become aware of many threats and hazards and have started to give serious thought to ways to prevent them.

Though I do not wish to detract from the importance of this achievement, I must say that very little or absolutely nothing has been done to solve most of the global problems that have been identified. We have been lucky enough insofar as this has not yet led to a universal disaster, though mankind has had to suffer staggering calamities of "local" wars, hunger, misery—misfortunes that have affected millions upon millions of people in various regions. But even this relative "luck" cannot last forever.

Therefore, in thinking about the coming twenty years, one cannot help arriving at the conclusion that this period may turn tragic if we limit our endeavors only to the realization and discussion of problems and fail to launch a process of really radical practical solutions. This should be one of the main characteristic features of the forthcoming twenty-year period; this should really distinguish it.

This is particularly true of the problems bearing on the military aspects of security, that is, the problems of prevention of nuclear war. This is a field in which science and technology, with the capacities and art of policy-making lagging badly behind, have brought matters to an extremely dangerous point. Many years ago it was universally recognized that an all-out nuclear conflict would be a disaster which would either wholly destroy modern civilization or hurl it back to a primitive stage. The realization of this fact has roused powerful forces of self-preservation which form the basis of the policy of détente, the policy that is aimed at the prevention of war.

In the last few years marked progress has been made along these lines. At the same time we have found that, though we have been promoting relaxation of tensions in the political sphere, though we have extended mutually advantageous cooperation in different areas, we have been unable to stem the arms race.

This phenomenon, that is, the phenomenon of relative independence of the arms race, which has been practically unaffected by changes in political relations, is an object of the present discussion. Some people maintain that this is due to unrestrained development of science and technology per se, that goes its own way and evades political control and, therefore, forces its will on military strategy and policy.

There might be a grain of truth in this. However, it seems that this phenomenon is not so much due to science and technology themselves but rather to the fact that political institutions and methods envisaged to exercise control over science and technology have remained to a large extent in the "prenuclear" stage and thus fail to meet the challenge in both scope and character.

This largely stems from developments that became obvious many years ago. One of these was that the huge war machine, unprecedently large for peace time, brought forces to life which, out of obvious vested interest, are seeking to preserve and expand it further. The economic system of the West has endowed these forces with great political influence. As a result, policy failed to effect control over the dynamics of arms production. What actually took place was militarization of policy-making and its subordination to the interests of the military-industrial complex. As to the second development, this is the heritage of the Cold War in political thinking and political behavior which has made it possible with relative ease to play on false or invented fears and thus secure support for (or, in any case, to undermine resistance to) the most dangerous and irrational decisions.

Other factors could be added to these. But this does not alter the heart of the matter, because a situation in which the race of armaments persists, despite détente and improvement of Soviet-American relations, is a very dangerous situation.

From the political point of view it is dangerous because it can foil or inhibit political détente and thus further intensify the arms race.

The economic aspect is a source of equally deep anxiety. If we extrapolate the growth of military expenditure in the past two decades and project it into the future, we shall obtain amounts that may jeopardize the very possibility of normal functioning of the economics of many countries, even those considered to be the richest, not excluding the United States.

The military aspect of the problem merits special attention, being intrinsically connected with the issue of security. From this point of view the coming two decades may well become critical. The continuation of keen military rivalry between the U.S.S.R. and the U.S.A., between the NATO countries and the Warsaw Treaty member states, creates a general situation that cannot fail to step up the threat of proliferation of nuclear weapons. I would not wish the acknowledgment of this truth to sound as justification for the course that might be taken by those statesmen and governments who might opt for nuclear armaments. Regardless of the circumstances, such a choice will be bad and dangerous. Far from promoting the security of any country and international security in general, such a decision will harm it. But this does not relieve of responsibility the powers that have already become nuclear, especially the United States and the Soviet Union; if they fail to control the arms race, the proliferation of nuclear weapons will become more probable.

It is also important to see other facets of the problem. If the nuclear powers are aware of the perilous consequences resulting from the proliferation of nuclear weapons, if they really wish to prevent this threat, it will not be enough for them to cooperate in strengthening the nonproliferation regime or even in curbing the arms race they are engaged in . They must also undertake joint effort to improve the entire international situation, to eliminate the foci of tensions, because their very existence increases the probability of appearance of more and more members of the "nuclear club."

Though the problem of proliferation of nuclear weapons is a very serious one, the threat of war created by the arms race is no longer limited to it alone. The past two decades give some idea of the tremendous expansion—both quantitative and qualitative—of military arsenals that may take place in such a span of time. But here the method of simple extrapolation will not produce an adequate picture of the development. In the last two decades the development of strategic weapon systems proceeded—with certain deviations and enormous redundancy—along the line of ensuring deterrence and improving its reliability. Though I haven't the least intention of idealizing the idea of deterrence, we can say that deterrence created a situation of a strategic impasse which helped up till now to avoid a nuclear conflict.

However, casting a glance at the next decade or two we shall have to admit that, if the arms race (both quantitative and qualitative) continues

at the present rate, it will not be reduced to deterrent alone and will play
an increasingly destabilizing role. This trend obviously manifested itself in
the late 1960s through early 1970s. If the Soviet-American agreements of
1972–1974 helped to stop one of the destabilizing systems (ABM), in another case the genie was allowed to escape from the bottle and, judging by
the circumstances, without hope of recovery.

I mean the MIRV systems. Regardless of the reasons produced by the
United States to justify this system at the time, its appearance caused an
increase in the number of nuclear warheads that widely exceeded the requirements of deterrence. The war planners lost no time in seeking ways to
utilize the "redundant" warhead, that is, finding newer and newer appropriate targets for them. Thus the idea of counterforce employment of strategic weapons has reintroduced at a new and more dangerous level.

It is difficult to conceive of a situation in which future programs would
be restricted to the limits of necessary deterrent. On the contrary, these
programs will rather promote trends initiated by the MIRV systems, trends
toward the creation of counterforce capabilities. Such is the purpose of
many programs already underway.

One cannot fail to see that taken as a whole these developments may
have far-reaching consequences in destabilizing the strategic situation,
imparting a new impulse to fears about disarming first-strike capability.
Thus, the foreseeable trends in the arms race will increase the risk of a possible acute international crisis leading to a tragic and irrevocable error.

I wish I could sincerely believe that all of the aforementioned is excessively tied to the polemics of the mid-1970s and will not appear so crucial
in ten or twenty years, because détente will have played the positive role
we expect it to play. However, the events may take a totally different
course. Science and technology are making such strides that one cannot
rule out the emergency of dangers that are even now difficult to foresee.

I would like to draw attention to another threat. The arms race may
proceed (and in certain cases it is already proceeding) along lines that will
make it more difficult or even impossible to conclude new agreements on
limitation and reduction of armaments, because they will put up insur-
mountable obstacles for verification. One of the negative consequences of
the appearance of strategic cruise missile stems herefrom.

Summing up, I would like to emphasize that the continued arms race
undoubtedly increases the danger of nuclear war, even though none of the
governments wants such war or is planning it deliberately.

What can and should be done to curb the arms race, the strategic arms
race above all? Just like every long and difficult path, the solution starts

with the first step. In today's circumstances this first step may—and really ought to—amount to the conclusion of the SALT II treaty. As to that, both sides, it seems, are in agreement.

But they do basically disagree as to the approach to the subject matter of such a treaty; to be more exact—as to whether or not the latter should be based on the Vladivostok accord. From our point of view it appears now to be very important to perceive that there just isn't and can hardly be another acceptable basis for the SALT II agreement. Today's conditions, embracing all the complexities of the strategic balance that implies a number of essential asymmetries, simply preclude progress toward more comprehensive agreements on arms limitations and reduction unless we start with the posture envisaged in Vladivostok and take account of all the complexities.

I in no way mean that the Vladivostok accord solves every problem of strategic arms race limitations and constitutes the utmost limit which is not to be trespassed. It is far from being so. To this effect, the Soviet Union introduced a number of proposals that do go beyond the Vladivostok accord. Neither do we give up our final goal: that of complete and general disarmament.

Still, the SALT II treaty must be centered around what was achieved in Vladivostok and negotiations that followed it. Recent Soviet-American talks in Moscow confirmed it in their own way.

Incidentally, I may as well mention that the American so-called comprehensive proposal introduced during these talks was rejected not because the Russians could not comprehend it quickly enough and properly appreciate it but precisely because the "package" was understood too well— understood as violating the initial premise of equality and providing for United States one-sided advantages.

The conclusion of the SALT II agreement—and I still hope that we shall witness it in not too long a time—will open up the possibilities for solution of other important tasks in the coming years. This might be really a decisive period. It seems that we could actually set ourselves the purpose to avoid approaching such a period of instability in the strategic situation to curb the arms race, to start the process of reduction of mass annihilation weapons. This could constitute the core of the SALT III and possibly of negotiations on other important new agreements, including, for instance, a ban on new types and systems of weapons of mass destruction.

It appears that, if the Soviet-American dialogue on arms limitations is furthered in the coming years, the parties should pay supreme attention to those developments in military technology and strategic concepts that constitute a special threat to strategic stability and to the preservation of peace. They include, for instance, the expansion of counterforce capabilities, the development of weapons systems that might obstruct the present and future arms limitation agreements, and all actions capable of contributing to the proliferation of nuclear weapons.

It will, apparently, be also timely and useful to look for ways to reach an understanding on problems bearing on the cardinal principles of strategic relationship of two countries, principles of military détente. These may be an enlargement upon the basic principles of mutual relations between the U.S.S.R. and the U.S.A. which have already been agreed upon. (I refer to such principles as the right to equal security, the commitment not to seek unilateral advantages, and the other provisions laid down in the agreement on the prevention of nuclear war.)

I have been dealing with strategic arms limitations although some other questions of military détente are undoubtedly just as important. I mean the limitation of armed forces and armaments in Central Europe, non-proliferation of nuclear weapons, limitation of the race of naval armaments (including such regions as the Indian Ocean and the Mediterranean), trade in arms, and so forth. All these spheres are fraught with mounting dangers, and this calls for quick and radical measures to prevent them from assuming proportions that would turn them into a threat to universal peace.

Success in these issues could make it possible further on to approach the solution of long-term mission, the gist of which may be defined as devising a system of measures aimed at actually separating foreign policy and national security issues from reliance on nuclear weapons and in the long run at renouncing and abolishing the latter altogether. Along with nuclear disarmament, steps should be undertaken toward limitation and reduction of the armed forces and of conventional armaments which, by the way, will become more and more unconventional if nothing is done to prevent it.

Since we are thinking about the coming two decades, I shall risk suggesting that twenty years ought to be sufficient to make key moves toward these goals, if even not to attain them fully. Otherwise, I very much fear that mankind will enter the third millenium under highly unfavorable auspices.

Whatever aspect of arms limitation we take up—the issues of today or the ones relating to the long-term future—one of the fundamental matters remains that of mutual confidence. It must be promoted and nourished, and we must carefully abstain from everything that might harm it.

Unfortunately, such an attitude has not yet been achieved to this day. To cite an example, one has only to think of the common American practice of hysterical campaigns about "military threat" coming allegedly from the other side. One of the features of détente, which distinguishes it from the Cold War, is that either side, if worried about the actions of the partner, can take up the matter directly at the required level through appropriate channels (and before the whole thing is allowed to "leak out" into the press).

I would prefer to formulate the question of confidence, of creating a political atmosphere that would be favorable for the solution of big international problems even in broader terms. I am opposed to the conception of "linkage" which was popular in U.S. policy at one time. You cannot make the solution of one difficult problem dependent on the preliminary solution of another problem, often not less difficult than the first one.

At the same time it would be naive to think that you can make progress in the solution of difficult and important problems, while charging the atmosphere with hostility and mistrust. This fully refers to the current anti-Soviet campaign speculating on civil rights issues.

I would not wish this remark to be understood as if I am against solicitude for human rights. Interest in this theme in itself cannot give rise to the objections, especially if the term is understood in its full and broad meaning. I wish to emphasize this point, because the current campaign in the West has grossly distorted this question, reduced it mainly to the right to emigrate and to engage in hostile activity against the existing system in the U.S.S.R. and other socialist countries.

In my opinion, everything that is being discussed in this series of lectures has bearing on human rights. The foremost right, naturally, is the right of physical existence, that is, the right of man to live in conditions of peace. Then as far as the overwhelming majority of mankind is concerned, the entire complex of economic and social rights is just as important as the political rights—the right to a job that would provide a standard of life worthy of man, the right to education and medical service, subsistence in old age, and access to the benefits of modern culture. Human rights organically include equality of nations and nationalities; they rule out any possibility of discrimination on grounds of race or nationality. Even the problem of the rights and freedoms that have served as a pretext for the present anti-Soviet campaign in the West is not so simple. I invite anybody to name a society in which they are not regulated in one way or another. And this is quite understandable, because of the eternal question of the bounds with which the freedom of the individual does not violate the rights and freedoms of other people and the well-being of society. The American approach to the settlement of this question is by no means acceptable to all. It has given rise to numerous disputes in the United States itself.

Therefore, if you take a look at the problem of human rights from a broader angle, you will see that the United States and the other Western countries are hardly justified in adopting the role of "moral policemen of the world." Different societies have different criteria of values and each side will uphold its ideas and conceptions. But there natural clashes of opinion should not be permitted to grow over into a policy of pressures on other countries, into attempts made from the outside with a view to changing the internal system in these countries. The Cold War has shown us where this leads to.

Permit me now to deal with the so-called problem of North-South relations, relations between the economically developed and the developing countries. In my opinion, the problem has been formulated in the background paper in terms that are too broad for concrete analysis, not taking account of either the fundamental differences between the economically developed countries and the scope of their concrete obligations to given countries of the Third World or diversity of the developing countries themselves. Nevertheless, I shall try to state a few considerations along the general lines laid down in the background paper. I am in agreement with the anxiety voiced in the paper with respect to the problems that arise in the widening gap between the rich and poor nations. I also agree that this gap must be closed as quickly as possible.

But permit me to make one reservation. As an exponent of the Marxist-Leninist social theory, I cannot remain silent about the fact that in my view it will be impossible to solve this, like many other problems, satisfactorily along traditional lines supported by the Western view, which means without radical economic and sociopolitical changes.

Many people in the West maintain that the Third World can and should develop along the same road as their own countries, that is, with the help of free enterprise and corresponding political and social institutions. I think that this road offers no prospects for the overwhelming majority of the countries of the Third World, as far as closing the gap between the level of development of the rich and poor nations is concerned.

I am now leaving out the factor of time, for it took the West whole centuries to reach a high level of development. Furthermore, I am not mentioning the fact that during very important periods of history Western capitalism could make successful progress only by exploiting—directly or indirectly—the colonies. This road of development is also closed to the countries of the Third World.

But the main point today may even be a different one. It is a historical fact that the overwhelming majority of developing countries function within the sphere of Western economic relations that was shaped while they were going through the colonial or semicolonial period of their history and thus were molded into the role of agricultural and raw material-providing appendages to the industrial states. In my opinion, the fact that "the rich are becoming richer, and the poor are becoming poorer" does not form the heart of the crisis of these relations; it is only a *manifestation* of this crisis. The gist of the matter is that the interests of development of the countries of the Third World are in contradiction with the system of economic relations to which these countries now belong.

It is becoming more and more obvious now that attempts to solve the problems of the developing countries solely with the help of financial and technological means have failed. The failure was due not only and not so much to the limited efforts and resources committed, but rather to the one-sided, narrow approach the West displayed to the complicated multi-faceted problems of the Third World.

If we take, for instance, a close look at the often impressive figures of Western aid to the developing countries, we will see that in some cases this aid boils down to the poor of the rich countries helping the rich in the poor countries. This sad phenomenon is observed not only in its primitive form, when foreign aid is used for building swimming pools of gold and for buying Mercedes cars and Cadillacs but also in the more sophisticated form when massive military aid is granted to keep reactionary regimes in power, regimes that bear exactly the same relation to economic progress in their countries as Humpty-Dumpty or "Alice in Wonderland" might to the world rope-walking champion.

Of course, to furnish a cardinal solution to development problems of the Third World, it is necessary to grant increasing aid to the developing countries and to provide a worthy place for them in the international organizations. In our opinion, however, these measures alone will not secure the desired solution. At present the question of creating a new economic order has been put on the agenda. I shall not attempt to discuss its contours in detail. One thing is clear, however: an economic order built on the rigid principles of the system of relations created by the West and dominated by the West will not help to close the gap between the poor and rich nations.

To overcome economic backwardness, poverty, misery, and hunger in the countries of the Third World in a short time, it is necessary to work radical changes in international economic relations. Changes that would help the developing countries find a worthy place in the system of international division of labor, take advantage of the achievements of scientific and technological progress, and build up a modern, diversified economy.

I do not want my words to be construed as speaking against the participation of private capital, including foreign private capital, in the development of the "Third" and "Fourth" World countries. We do see that private capital has a role to play and that role might be a useful one. But that usefulness is limited, it is but an auxiliary force, and that with the prerequisite of national control of the economy.

Even highly developed countries find it increasingly difficult to rely on the free play of the economic forces; the government finds it necessary to amend and to guide the private sector. This is still more relevant if one turns to the developing countries which face most complicated tasks to be solved under the condition of extreme scarcity of many—if not all—resources.

Today, not only theoretical appraisal but also practical experience (including that of the countries once considered to be working "economic miracles") lead us to the conclusion that it is totally inadequate to measure the progress of the developing countries exclusively in terms of the GNP growth. The core of the problem is to achieve comprehensive progress that will not only narrow the gap in the general level of economic development but will also radically change the fate of the majority of the population, solving most acute social problems. Experience proves that this is usually not the case. There are countries boasting rather rapid growth, but this growth results in making only 5 to 7 percent of the population richer while 90 percent remain in miserable condition or even become still more impoverished—if that is possible.

And there is another important point. The problem of development is above all the problem of choosing the optimal road of development. In our opinion, which is confirmed by the experience of development of the Central Asian and Transcaucasian republics of our country whose economic level was about the lowest among the regions of Russia, the optimal road of development is the noncapitalist road. Voicing this opinion, we do not want to force on the young states one road of development or another. It is up to every state to make the choice.

As far as the above points are concerned, the East and the West maintain different views. And it is difficult to expect them to draw closer to one another to any considerable degree. Though there are differences on these points, it does not follow that the developed countries—both capital-ist and socialist—cannot join efforts in assisting the Third World in solving important problems of development. Here, too, I would like to point above all to the profound connections between the global problems of development and those of international détente. By advancing along the road of détente, we could create a more favorable international climate to search for ways to solve the fundamental problems of development. For instance, it would create a practical possibility for ending the so-called poor man's arms race, that is, the grossly irrational situation when huge sums of money badly needed for purposes of development are spent by countries of the Third World on extremely costly modern weapons.

Certainly one has to have a clear idea of the reasons that push the poor countries toward purchasing arms. Quite often these reasons include real threats to their independence and national security or the existence of hotbeds of international tensions in different regions of the world. Thus, curbing the poor man's arms race implies not only agreement on limitation of arms trade among the countries that do sell armaments but also im-provement of regional political climates and peaceful settlement of local conflicts.

In conditions of détente, it becomes quite possible to use much more effectively for development the aggregate scientific and technological re-sources of mankind such as the material results of joint investigations in global problems and joint efforts to utilize the resources of the world ocean.

As far as programs of economic, scientific, and technical assistance are concerned, they can, no doubt, play a big role. But the case of such a wonderful undertaking as the "green revolution" shows that very much here depends on the economic and social conditions in the developing countries themselves. This example has again shown that problems bearing on the acceleration of the development of the Third World are in one way or another connected with the removal of backward social structures.

Also, I would like to point out that in case we manage to curb military spending the developed countries would be increasingly willing to make larger allocations to help countries of the Third and Fourth World to over-come their backwardness. And, on the contrary, these allocations will drop if military spending rises. The effectiveness of the efforts the developed countries will make to aid the developing countries will also depend on their ability to establish cooperation with one another in the execution of a number of global programs.

And now permit me to touch upon the problems of resources. I shall not

repeat what the background paper says on the matter. In the main I share
the views set forth in it particularly on the need for international cooperation in the solution of many aspects of this problem, including scientific
and technical cooperation. In the long-term perspective, scientific and
technological progress alone can offer a way out of the difficulties created
by contemplated raw material shortages.

The Soviet Union is prepared to take part in such cooperation, and this
was again confirmed by L. I. Brezhnev at the Twenty-fifth Congress of our
party:

Global problems such as primary materials and energy, the eradication of
the most dangerous and widespread diseases, environmental protection,
space exploration and the utilization of the resources of the World Ocean
are already sufficiently important and urgent. In the future they will exercise an increasingly perceptible influence on the life of each nation and on
the entire system of international relations. The Soviet Union, like other
socialist countries, cannot hold aloof from the solution of these problems
which affect the interest of all mankind.

The problem of resources being a global one, it naturally has a physical
aspect (that is, limited supply of these resources in nature) and also a
social one. The role of the latter is often underestimated. However, it is
difficult to refrain from giving this aspect priority in the solution of the
entire problem.

It would be sufficient to mention the role the international oil corporations played in creating the preconditions for the so-called oil crisis to
show that the problem of resources today is to a great degree a problem of
controlling the corporate interests that often contradict the national and
even international interests.

Similarly, the problem of hunger in many of the developing countries is
not one of the world community failing to produce enough food but
rather one of the existing social mechanism preventing adequate production and distribution of food supplies.

The whole issues of more economical utilization of natural resources is
closely connected with the social aspect of the problem. In this connection
I would like to return to the topic of the arms race and look into it from
another angle.

A short while ago I saw an American estimate in which it was said the
planned fleet of B-1 bombers would consume 25 billion gallons of fuel in
25 years. This is far more than all the urban public transportation systems
in the U.S.A. will consume over the same period. This figure urged me to
give thought to the question, How much fuel does the whole war machine
of the world devour? How much aluminum, steel, copper, and all sorts of

other materials that are now in short supply are being expended on the building and maintenance of this machine?

Permit me to raise another question in the connection. The world now is generously expending for military aims the most valuable of all resources of mankind—the brain potential. According to some estimates, out of every thousand scientists and engineers about two hundred are working in the military sphere. Now that we are being faced with an increasing number of problems, including the problem of "the governability of complexity" listed in the background paper, we can ask ourselves the question: Can we afford such extravagances in the future?

In conclusion, all of this makes me return to the influence of the international situation on the possibility of solving the problems confronting mankind; more specifically, to the importance of détente.

Détente itself does not solve all the problems. Far from it. However, without détente, that is, without peace, arms limitation, improvement of the international situation, broad development of mutually advantageous cooperation, we shall not be able even to proceed with the solution of almost all of the problems listed for discussion in this series of lectures.

As I see it, the key element of policy for the future—whether it is only for next year or for the next twenty years—will be the preservation, advancement, and consolidation of détente. The influence exercised by the global problems we discussed on international relations will depend on this. In conditions of tensions, hostility, and unrestricted rivalry, this influence might prove to be destructive; it may lead to more and more new conflicts. In conditions of détente, the need to solve global problems may cement relations between the peoples, may serve as a powerful incentive for cooperation and as its motive force. Therefore, this need may become a vital factor of international security.

8

Africa's Moral Imperatives:
Liberation, Identity,
Humanness

Canon Burgess Carr

Africa needs a new type of citizen: a dedicated, modest, human, informed
man. A man who submerges himself in service to his nation and mankind.
A man who abhors greed and detests vanity. A new type of man whose
humanity is his strength and whose integrity is his greatness.
Kwame Nkrumah

I have used this quotation in homage to the man I regard as Africa's leading citizen of our generation. As dreamer, visionary, and strategist of the
African Revolution, Kwame Nkrumah, more than any other single individual, was the prime mover of the forces that have plunged Africa into the
sea of cataclysmic changes. In invoking his memory, I am conscious that
1977 marks the twentieth anniversary of the independence of Ghana. In
this lecture, I intend to reflect upon the aspirations and expectations that
event inspired within the African peoples one generation ago. Then I want
to show that Africa's contribution to world peace and security over the
next decades, lay in the achievement of our struggle for *liberation, identity, and humanness.*

Poised Between Drums and Slums

It was Arnold Toynbee who said that future historians will identify the
great event of the twentieth century as "the impact of Western civilization
upon all other living societies of the world of that day. They will say," he
went on, "that it was so powerful and so pervasive that it turned the lives
of all its victims upside down and inside out—affecting the behavior, outlook, feelings and beliefs of individual men, women and children in an intimate way, touching cords in human souls that are not touched by mere
external, material forces—however ponderous and terrifying."[1] Of no part
of the world can this be said with greater global accuracy than of Africa.

However, to speak of the impact of Western civilization upon Africa, is to speak about colonialism.

Colonialism in Africa involves economic exploitation, racial oppression, and cultural violence. These three aspects have produced a situation of disequilibrium in our societies from which we are still struggling to liberate ourselves. It has been and still is a long, hard struggle.

In retrospect, we would call it our struggle of the century. It has been militantly waged ever since the first generation of this century, when the mystique of *blackness and liberation* combined to form the political ideology of *Pan-Africanism.* The seminal ideas of Pan-Africanism continue to be the leitmotif of our age-old struggle.

[We] believe in peace. How could it be otherwise, when for centuries the African peoples have been the victims of violence and slavery? Yet if the Western world is still determined to rule mankind by force, then Africans, as a last resort, may have to appeal to force in the effort to achieve freedom, even if force destroys them and the world.

We are determined to be free. We want education. We want the right to earn a decent living; the right to express our thoughts and emotions, to adopt and create forms of beauty.

We demand for Black Africa autonomy and independence . . .

We are not ashamed to have been an age-long patient people. We continue willingly to sacrifice and to strive. *But we are unwilling to starve any longer while doing the world's drudgery in order to support by our poverty and ignorance a false aristocracy and a discarded imperialism.*

We condemn the monopoly of capital and the rule of private wealth and industry for private profit alone. We welcome economic democracy, as the only real democracy.

Therefore we will continue to complain, appeal and arraign. We will make the world listen to the facts of our condition. We will fight in every way we can for freedom, democracy and social betterment.[2]

Our struggle for *freedom, democracy, and social betterment* continues. But today it is a struggle waged not only against external domination, as important as that remains, but equally against those forces and structures through which Africans themselves have internalized the values and lifestyles of their alien oppressors. We must speak about this here because this is the utterly ridiculous dilemma undermining the African Revolution.

Based on the ideology of Pan-Africanism, Nkruma's strategy for the African Revolution involved three phases: the first was liberation from colonial rule, to be followed by the consolidation of political independence, and, thirdly, the social transformation of independent African states. Over the last twenty years, we have made tremendous strides in the first phase, as the "winds of change blowing through Africa" swept away alien rule until it was arrested at the Zambezi. With the exception of Algeria and Kenya the process of political decolonization involved a nonviolent consti-

tutional devolution of power. However, it was this very fact that check-
mated the drive to consolidate our political independence and to achieve
the social transformation of our nations.

Two features of the devolutionary process are worth mentioning in this
connection. First, the instruments of sovereignty, that is, territorial boundaries, constitutions, governmental structure and machinery, etc. did not
allow for the social and political traditions indigenous to Africa. There are
many cynics who now contend that this was so by design, in order to create conditions in which the myth about the innate incapability of Africans
to govern themselves could be perpetuated. We shall examine this in due
course.

The second feature of the change from colonial rule to self-government
was the stubborn determination of the colonial powers that whatever else
independence would mean—flag, national anthem, titles, what have you—
one thing it would not mean: the cutting loose of Africa from the capitalist world. Colonialism was the indispensable handmaid of capitalism, and if
colonialism in its traditional form was no longer fashionable, neocolonial
strategies had to be contrived in order to ensure that Africa remained within the orbit of the capitalist world.

To achieve this, a capitalist class of indigenous Africans had to be created who would identify with the interests of the colonialists. But how
does one transform primary school teachers and junior civil servants into a
comprador bourgeois class in a single generation? By providing opportunity for them to become corrupt and amass instant, ill-gotten wealth. This
process has resulted in the pervasive corruption that eats like a cancer at
the heart of all our nations.

Because they fear the hatred and rage that their corrupt practices have
aroused among their peoples, many African leaders are determined not to
relinquish power. The same fear is responsible for the concentration of
political and economic power in the hands of a tiny elitist group; for the
arbitrary detention of dissidents, imaginary or real; for the diverting of
public funds from development programs that would benefit the entire
population to the operations of diabolical propaganda machinery and
secret police units called by various names and having unlimited powers to
terrorize, murder, and massacre the population.

This process of substituting alien colonial rule with a neocolonial local
oligarchy, has produced widespread instability in Africa. More than a million men, women, and children are now refugees and their numbers are
increasing every day. The healthy hopes of twenty years ago are still-born;
our national economies are more precarious; ostentatious living is flagrant

among the privileged elite; the moral authority of governments is under-
mined and eroded every time someone holding a controversial point of
view "disappears"* and nobody seems to care. In a word, we are poised
between the life-giving rhythm of our traditional drumbeats and the de-
humanizing squalor of the urban slums.

Cultural Genocide

Our present state of affairs would never have arisen if Africans and their
cultures had not been placed unjustly under the yoke of mockery and
derision. The worst damage to Africa is not the economic plunder of our
wealth and resources. It is, rather, the plunder of our souls. Our colonizers,
having first alienated us from our human house, have recreated us elites in
their own image and likeness. In so doing, their prolonged influence is assured, even though they themselves may not be physically present.

Nowhere is this fact more in evidence than in the Christian Church in
Africa. There is ample evidence to demonstrate that African peoples who
had repelled European invasion found themselves amenable to subjugation
after they had been *christianized* by missionaries. It comes as no surprise,
then, that "organized Christianity is identified with the political and economic exploitation of the . . . African people by alien powers."[3]

The objective goals of the African Revolution can therefore only be
achieved through cultural liberation that will rescue African values, history,
and culture from the state of ridicule and disdain they have suffered for
so long.

In the All Africa Conference of Churches, we are attempting to liberate
the Churches from the religious-cultural imperialism of their missionary
mentors. Essentially, we believe that as long as the Church in Africa remains in captivity to an alien theological world view and its cultural lifestyles, it can make no contribution to the liberation of Africa from
domination and dependence. Therefore we have called for a *moratorium*
on expatriate personnel and funds to the Church in Africa, in order that
African Christians can discover for themselves ways of bringing Africa's
own religious treasures to enrich the Christian faith. Furthermore, we have
initiated programs of study and research on the integration of early Christianity with the cultures of ancient Egypt and Ethiopia, where churches
have survived from the time of the first Apostles until this day. We believe
there is much to learn from these ancient churches that would be helpful
to the *missionary-established* and *African independent* churches in their

Disappearance is a euphemism for assassination by government law enforcement
units like the "State Research Bureau" in Uganda.

search for authentically African forms of worship, discipline, theology, and administration.

Having said this it is appropriate to answer the question: Who is an African? Is African cultural identity a tangible or an intangible reality? By African culture I mean those linguistic, ecological, political, religious, and aesthetic features with which we, as a race of men and women, are peculiarly endowed, and which are repeatedly ours in time and space. Call it our *esse*, if you like. It is that cluster of values epitomized in our unity with otherness; our unity with our human past, and our unity with nature.

This intrinsic unity defines the two aspects of the African personality namely a "me" and a "communal me" or a "me in communion." There does exist a "me" which is the vital principle linked to a body with its temporal destiny. But far more important is the "me in communion" that is in living contact with the cosmos and by which the union of life and the seeds of passage—the vital link between the dead, the living and the unborn—is perpetually assured. African cultural identity confirms the African personality as living-in-relation. It confirms our perception of the world as a holistic and unitary reality, where life has primacy over death, and the force of the spirit constitutes a rhythm of intensive continuity. On the existential plane, it also confirms the value of collective responsibility for communal ownership of the earth.

Derived from this *Weltanschauung* are sociopolitical and economic constraints that determine societal organizations and control. These are specifically manifested in our modes of living, our social structure, and our ways of maintaining control over our human and material environment so as to ensure life and prosperity. A moment ago I referred to the total absence of any of these uniquely African sociopolitical concepts in the instruments of sovereignty which form the basis of our new nations. There are two such concepts that come readily to mind.

The first may be described as "integratedness," by which I mean our people's perception of their political leader as the embodiment and spirit of the collective will and unity of the entire society. The other, I will call "integrity," a system through which checks and balances are devised to control the role of government. Government symbolizes the collective unity of society, not the right of various ruling groups, like heads of households or clans, to infringe upon the rights of the people or to jeopardize the welfare of society as a whole.

These concepts of "integratedness" and "integrity" are complementary. As custodians of communal power, political authority in traditional African society was sustained by a system of reciprocal responsibility. In order for government to function smoothly, there had to be a balance between the claims and demands of the ruler and expectations of the ruled. As the symbol of the will and spirit of his people and the focal point of all that concerned the welfare and stability of society, the traditional ruler was regarded as *father* and *protector.* All of the privileges and power he enjoyed were placed in his hands in faith and trust that as *father* and *protector* he would defend his people against internal unrest and external attack; and, through propitiation of the ancestors, he would ensure the good health, well-being, and prosperity of society. In short, people paid homage and allegiance to their rulers and provided them with goods and services in return for spiritual and physical protection. Ideally the system of reciprocal responsibility assured that political authority was not misused for personal ends.

These essential considerations have been brushed aside, and we are attempting to create new models of society based on an alien world view. Traditional concepts of unity, communality, integratedness, and integrity have been replaced by the fierce pursuit of individuality, privacy, and personal wealth. The result is the sort of cultural schizophrenia that leaves us bewildered and frustrated. The task of the future is to recover continuity by linking our precolonial past to the postcolonial present. That is why *the struggle continues!*

Liberation Beyond Independence

There is widespread consensus that the political institutions inherited from our colonial mentors are woefully inadequate to fulfill the authentic aspirations of our peoples. The alternatives so far introduced have not filled the need either. Beyond an apparent stability, which in very many cases is ruthlessly maintained in order to attract and protect foreign economic interest, there exists widespread unrest and a deep sense of insecurity. Military rule and/or one party states appear as nothing other than euphemisms for authoritarianism at best and repression at worst. Ideological labels, like "socialist" and "revolutionary" in most cases are cover-ups for elitest rule or a new sort of caste system which excludes the vast majority of the people from participation in decision-making. In a country like Ethiopia today, "socialist" or "marxist" is a euphemism for mayhem and revenge, and in equatorial Guinea and Uganda, "revolutionary" means massacres, harassment, torture, and assassinations.

In highlighting these cases, I have no intention of downgrading the struggles in which we are engaged for the higher interests of Africa— the end to

white racist domination and economic exploitation. It should be clear
from what I have said about the emergence of an African *capitalist* elite
class that I regard the internal repression of our people by our own leaders
as an extension of the persistent colonial intransigence in Africa. It is essential to remember what I have said about the Western colonial powers'
determination to keep Africa within the capitalist orbit. As I see it, the
new imperialist strategy is one of establishing subimperialist centers in
southern, eastern, central, north, and west Africa, from which the rest of
the continent can be controlled. From this perspective, I regard the racist
regimes in southern Africa, as well as most of the one party states and military regimes in the rest of Africa as children from the womb of the same
mother—imperialism.

In this context the armed liberation struggle against colonial rule won by
by the people of Guinea Bissau, Angola, and Mozambique, and still being
waged today by the peoples of Azania, Namibia, and Zimbabwe represents
a creative alternative to the attainment of independence by devolution.

The objective of the liberation movements is to create conditions in
which Africans assume the responsibility for bringing about change in their
situation under their own direction. The liberation struggle is therefore a
struggle to transform Africans from *objects* into *subjects.* It is being waged
in order that Africans themselves may have the right to determine the
tempo and texture of the changes required to achieve self-determination
and true independence.

The liberation struggle in southern Africa is not just about majority rule.
The liberation movements are convinced that armed struggle is the only
viable option left to them as a strategy for the total liberation of Azania,
Namibia, and Zimbabwe. Neither is the struggle in these countries any
longer one about civil rights, or about dismantling apartheid, or about
adjusting white attitudes and privileges to accommodate blacks. The armed
liberation struggle is a revolutionary process through which a new society
based on justice and solidarity is established. This is the reason that the
liberation movements reject any direct external intervention, whether it be
by Nigerians or Americans, Czechs, or Cubans. They want to fight their
own battles and win their own victories.

Today, the masses of the African people support the liberation movements because they are simultaneously waging the struggle against colonial
domination, consolidating the gains of their struggle, and attempting to
transform their societies. The goal is no longer flag-waving independence,
but *authentic, total liberation.* Hence, Africans identify in the liberation
struggle their own unfulfilled aspirations and expectations of a generation

ago. This is made manifest in the militancy and pervasive revolts of students everywhere on the continent. From Cairo to the Cape, from
Morocco to Malagasy, the indictment of the students against the first generation of postcolonial leaders is the same: *We placed the reins of our
world in your hands, but you have plunged it over a precipice into an
abyss of despair.*

Fairness demands, however, that we acknowledge the constraints imposed upon contemporary African leaders who are called upon to squeeze
centuries into decades. Not for us is the relaxed tempo of countries which
built their economies in an earlier and more tranquil age without having to
dismantle colonial institutions, countries which could be content with
gradual reform and the steady workings of social change. In one generation
we are trying to create an environment of opportunity, an ethos of equality, and a destiny of dignity for the underprivileged majority of our
peoples.

There are those, like President Nyerere of Tanzania, who cheerfully
undertake the toil and sweat for a better life for the masses; who accept
the denial of immediate comfort; who live on a thin margin. But the values
of our sacrifices are constantly jeopardized by institutions and practices
that structurally operate against us. The currency of our labor and toil is
retrogressively devalued by unequal economic relations between the richer,
affluent, industrialized countries and ourselves. The global economic crisis
of the mid-seventies resulting from the accelerated increases in the price of
oil, for instance, has had its worst impact on us and retarded our development by many years. In some countries, like Kenya where I live, balance-
of-payments imperatives oblige us to deny meat and milk to our children,
who are suffering from malnutrition, in order that these products may be
available for export. In Liberia, my own country, huge tracts of excellent
land are given to the production of rubber for export, in face of the massive threat of hunger and malnutrition prevailing in West Africa. We continue to complain and to appeal but, ironically, instead of evoking the
natural response of a sense of interdependence, there is increasingly visible
a pernicious self-righteousness among the rich. The traditional racist myths
concerning the inherent inferiority of African peoples persists and imputes
the blame for our plight on ourselves.

Shall We Make or Mar?

Confronted by this situation, Africa needs urgently to examine the integral
link between our collective weakness and our external economic and ideo-

logical relationships. It is imperative that we should forge fresh bonds of solidarity and interdependence. With the rich nations embarked on a course designed to strengthen their own groupings and associations, the survival of the weak nations of Africa depends entirely upon their unity.

Earlier this year in my New Year's message, I called upon the Organization of African Unity to set up a task force or think tank to develop strategy for the organic unity of Africa by 1984.[4] I warned that unless this happens it is very likely that by that year we will witness another partitioning of Africa by the superpowers and their surrogates. My appeal and warning are based upon my assessment of the ascendency of the forces of polarization over those of community and solidarity in Africa. The breakup of the East African Community represents one illustration from the *right;* while the current crisis in Zaire[5] represents an illustration from the *left,* in the prevailing ideological spectrum.

Perhaps there is validity to the view that it is imperative for obtuse structures of inequality to be abolished in order to make way for viable associations based on mutual respect, human dignity, and reciprocal sharing. I accept this on the fierce insistence that the movement toward creating the new should not be sabotaged by those strong currents bent on setting us back in our voyage to self-reliance and self-realization. This is a voyage we must make together in unity or we shall perish separately in the sea of dissidence, secession, and recolonization.

It is in this perspective that we urgently need to give consideration to expanding the concept of African Unity. Although the impetus was first launched in reference to the unity of Black men and women of African descent the world over, since the end of the Second World War the Pan-African ideology has been hijacked by the emergent African states and made to appear to be their exclusive prerogative. There are two unhappy consequences of this: First, nationalism as defined by territorial frontiers has fractured the cultural and other continuities that universally define the African personality; second, millions of Africans-in-diaspora are cut off from the emotions of belonging to their ancestral homeland. Efforts like those of Alex Haley will have to be matched by similar determination on the part of Africa's Africans to build bridges of solidarity through communications media, increased exchanges of visits by scholars and stevedores, domestics and doctors, and greater identity with the political and social aspirations of Africa and her peoples. It should come as no surprise if we maintain that first priority should be given to forging links of solidarity with those away from the shores of continental Africa with whom we share common spiritual, ancestral, and cultural roots.

Next we must strengthen our solidarity with other Third World peoples with whom we share a common heritage of colonial suffering and exploitation. In spite of every other consideration with regard to political system or external outlook, the Third World nations have a common mandate to extricate the world's majority from the stranglehold of domination and dependence. Here too our survival depends entirely upon collective effort.

Lest I be accused of advocating further polarization and confrontation between African and other Third World peoples on the one hand, and the rich, industrialized world on the other, I should like to make it clear that everything I have said in this regard is meant as a *response* to the blatant arrogance with which the rich, industrialized nations today deal with issues like international monetary reform, trade and resource flow, fluctuations in commodity prices, and ideological or military hegemony. In all these vital matters the influence of Africa and other Third World countries is tepid and peripheral.

Of course I do believe in interdependence between Africa and the rest of the world. Nowadays it is generally conceded in authoritative scholarly circles that humankind originated in Africa. This makes the African man *father* and the African woman *mother* of the entire human race. This fact alone imposes upon us an awesome stewardship for safeguarding the future of humankind. Shall we make or mar so solemn a responsibility? Which way Africa?

Here we stand
  Poised between two civilizations.
Backward
  To the days of drums and festal dances
  in the shade of sun-kist palms. Or forward
Toward
  The slums, where man is dumped upon man . . . .

These powerful lines by Dei-Anang capsulize the challenge we face in our voyage to self-fulfillment. We cannot remain standing, motionless. We need a synthesis between our past and our present. On balance, the past has left us a beneficial legacy of shared values and a humanistic culture. To a very large extent these values are still present and operational among the overwhelming majority of our peoples. Any synthesis we devise therefore must guarantee that the entire social order is changed in favor of the common man.

The Wager of Our Generation

It should be clear that I perceive the first task for Africa in the last quarter of this century to be *the total and complete elimination of colonialism in all its forms from our continent.* It is entirely inconceivable that after three hundred years of slavery and a century of colonial rule Africans can still be expected to tolerate continued alien domination and subjugation. We are determined to break this *eurocentric* syndrome that has engulfed our lives for so long.

Obviously, the larger issues related to neocolonialism cannot be tackled effectively as long as areas of Africa remain under alien immigrant rule. Therefore Africans have placed the highest priority upon the liberation struggle against colonialism and racism in southern Africa. As we see it, the persistence of these manifestations of direct foreign domination, apart from whatever else they represent, is an affront to the dignity and self-respect of black men and women the world over. As long as such naked domination of Africa by a tiny minority of racist settlers is tolerated, the entire African race is victimized by calumny and disdain.

The intransigence of the minority regimes in southern Africa, buttressed by the diplomatic, political, massive economic and strategic military support they receive from Western countries, is the greatest single threat to peace and security in the world today. Unless this situation changes radically, unless France, West Germany, and the United States desist forthwith from enabling South Africa to acquire nuclear capability, then we can be absolutely certain of a global race war in the next generation. And it might well be fought with nuclear weapons.

Given the massive developmental needs we face, Africans naturally would prefer to avoid such a conflict, and we have said so. After all, we are not anxious to move from subjugation to annihilation. We believe that we too are entitled to make our contribution to the universal fund of human values in tranquility. So we yearn for peace.

Precisely because we yearn for peace—precisely because as an entire race we are tired of oppression and plunder—we are totally committed to create conditions for the realization of greater human justice in our world. We are totally committed to eliminate violence—the structural violence of racial and colonial oppression as much as the social violence of economic, class, and political exploitation.

We reject any notions that limit the concept of violence to the response that oppressed people are obliged to make in face of massive repression and dehumanization. And this is the basis of my concept of *sanctified violence.* I believe that violence can be "sanctified" if it is used selectively, not for revenge and vengeance but as a means of liberating both the oppressed and their oppressors.

Of parallel importance to the task of eliminating colonialsim and its legacies from Africa is that of ensuring adequate protection of human rights. However, *human rights* must not be construed to mean *minority rights,* whether that minority is one of race or of class. Based on the communal interpretations of the African personality and society I have described, it is clear that Africa's conception of *human rights* will differ significantly from that derived from the nineteenth-century European preoccupation with the privacy of the individual. *Human rights in Africa must involve a greater regard for the group rights of society as a whole,* against the private rights of individuals or of classes.

Third, Africa shall have to develop alternative ways of changing governments, other than by assassinations and coup d'état. This can only be assured through a commitment to democratic methods. We shall have to create an atmosphere in which differences and honest disagreements can be faced openly. We shall have to build a climate for reconciliation and participation. But this will demand much greater responsiveness on the part of our leaders to the needs and longings of their peoples than have been evident up to the present time.

Fourth, security in Africa in the next decade will depend upon our capacity to create models of development that go beyond the material goals of modernization and economic progress. We need a concept of development based on the commitment to provide a decent life for the entire human society before any individual can be allowed to enjoy luxuries. Such a concept of development will inevitably derive much more from the communalistic tenets of traditional African society than from Western capitalism.

Therefore, I appeal to the Western capitalist nations to leave Africa alone, in order that we may develop not only our material well-being, but our human creativity and values as well.

Finally, I will repeat what I have already said. The organic unity of Africa is an urgent priority for the future. The world is moving into the Age of Globality. An Africa made up of a series of mini states risks becoming nothing more than client-vassal states of the more powerful nations. The organic unity of Africa is the only means of ensuring our sovereignty and safeguarding the achievements of our struggle for liberation.

The task of eliminating the legacy of colonialism, of creating democratic machinery to guarantee the broadest protection of human, political, and societal rights, of evolving patterns of development that are human-centered and the organic unity of African nations constitute the wager of our generation and yours.

I consider that in these tasks Africa deserves the enabling support and assistance of the United States of America and of its Western partners. Yours is the dominant political, economic, social, and neocultural influence on our continent. Other protagonists are new. However, these nations that you accuse of having hegemonic ambitions in Africa demonstrate greater sensitivity to our legitimate aspirations than you do. Why is this? We are bewildered and perplexed by your lack of meaningful support for values derived out of your own revolution, that we in Africa today find ourselves defending. Some of the vibrations we have felt in the first days of the Carter administration give cause for hope that American policy toward Africa may shift significantly in favor of justice and human rights. We hope we are not mistaken. The United States of America has leverages that no other nation in the world has over the minority, colonial regimes in South Africa and Southern Rhodesia. You have the capacity to talk to them and to us, something neither the Russians nor the Chinese can do. You have the largest black population away from the continent of Africa— a population larger than that of the vast majority of independent African nations. There is no way the United States can excuse herself if she reneges on her responsibility to assist Africa to make her contribution to the forward march of humankind.

Epilogue

As a man of religion and a Christian, I have spoken of Africa's struggle for liberation, identity, and humanness. I regard these to be moral imperatives and, as such, properly the concerns of the Christian Church.

Underlying everything I have said is my own deep, personal commitment to see African Christianity, enriched by the spiritual and moral genius in our religious heritage as much as by our own historical experience, restore spiritual consciousness and justice as the axis around which the affairs of existence and universal human purpose must turn. I am utterly convinced that the credibility of the Christian Church depends upon the prophetic vigor with which it exposes the moral delinquencies that militate against Africa's struggle for liberation, identity, and humanness. As a consequence, I believe that the mission of the African Church is to see to it that Christianity re-emerges as a dynamic and essentially revolutionary force of religious energy on the world scene. It is the breath of life to us that we fulfill this mission. Only thus will Africa make its unique contribution to world peace and security in the decades ahead; not only as the custodian of humanity's origins but, more importantly, as the steward of humanity's future.

Notes

1. "Civilization on Trial" in *Civilization on Trial and the World and the West* (Meredian, 1958), p. 189.

2. Resolution of the Pan-African Congress, Manchester 1945 in *Africa Yearbook* (Africa Journal Limited, 1976), p. 173.

3. *Op. cit.*

4. 1984 is one hundred years after the Congress of Berlin that partitioned Africa among the European colonial powers.

5. At the time of the essay, Zaire was waging a civil war against Katangese insurgents who had invaded the copper-rich Shaba Province from Angola.

9   The World Population Problem

Robert S. McNamara

Introduction

Nearly a dozen years ago, in the city of Montreal, I delivered an address—
as the U.S. Secretary of Defense—on the problems of international security.

My central point was that the concept of security itself had become
greatly oversimplified. There was an almost universal tendency to think of
the security problem as being exclusively a military problem, and to think
of the military problem as being exclusively a weapons-system or hardware
problem. "We still tend to conceive of national security," I noted, "almost
solely as a state of armed readiness: a vast, awesome arsenal of weaponry."

But, I pointed out, if one ponders the problem more deeply, it is clear
that force alone does not guarantee security and that a nation can reach a
point at which it does not buy more security for itself simply by buying
more military hardware. That was my view in 1966. It remains my view in
1977.

In a volatile, violent world, it is of course necessary for a nation to establish defense forces in order to protect itself. Such forces are always expensive, but if the funds are wisely used there is a reasonable ratio between
the amount of money spent and the degree of protection acquired. One
can graph that ratio as a curve. In the initial stages the curve arches upward, and security expands with expenditure. But as the spending grows
larger and larger, the curve inevitably begins to flatten out.

There is a point at which an additional dollar of defense simply no

I am indebted to a long list of distinguished scholars and specialists for much of
what follows. Their research and insights have assisted me immensely. In particular
I want to thank the members of the External Advisory Panel on Population who, at
my request, recently reviewed the World Bank's work in the population field. They
are: Bernard Berelson, Chairman; Ronald Freedman; Goran Ohlin; Frederick T. Sai;
and A. Chandra Sekhar.

longer buys an additional dollar's worth of security. Expenditures beyond that point are not only wasted on defense but will erode the funds available for other essential sectors. And by denying that dollar to other essential investment, the process may in the end diminish security rather than bolster it.

Now, if we examine defense expenditures around the world today—and measure them realistically against the full spectrum of components that tend to promote order and stability within and among nations—it is clear that there is a mounting misallocation of resources (Figure 1). We are far out on the flat of the curve.

That is true in the industrialized world. It is true as well in many parts of the developing world.

Global defense expenditures have become so large that it is difficult to grasp their full dimensions. The overall total is now in excess of $350 billion a year. The United States and the Soviet Union together account for some 60 percent of that—and for 75 percent of the world's arms trade. They possess more military power than all the other nations of the world combined.

And yet it is not in the industrialized countries but in the developing countries that military budgets are rising the fastest. As a group, the governments in the developing world are now spending as much for military programs as for education and health care combined.

If we are concerned—as all of us must be in this thermonuclear age— about international security, then we would do well to reconsider our present priorities. Do we really believe that we can turn the earth into a less violent place to live by an ever-increasing factor of force?

Is the ultimate objective somehow to armor-plate the entire planet?

The question is grotesque. And yet, not any more so than the premise

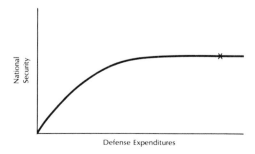

Defense Expenditures

Figure 1

on which much of the world's thinking about security appears to be based.

I want to discuss with you tonight a subject that has nothing whatever to do with military phenomena—but a very great deal to do with global tranquility. It is the issue of population growth. Short of thermonuclear war itself, it is the gravest issue the world faces over the decades immediately ahead. Indeed, in many ways rampant population growth is an even more dangerous and subtle threat to the world than thermonuclear war, for it is intrinsically less subject to rational safeguards, and less amenable to organized control.

The population growth of the planet is not in the exclusive control of a few governments, but rather in the hands of literally hundreds of millions of individual parents who will ultimately determine the outcome. That is what makes the population threat—even more than the nuclear threat— diffuse and intractable. And that is why it must be faced—like the nuclear threat—for what it inevitably is: both a central determinant of mankind's future, and one requiring far more attention of the world community than it is presently receiving.

What, then, I would like to do in this address is this:

examine the background of the population problem;

analyze its current trends;

evaluate the measures available to deal with it; and

suggest the actions that governments and others can and must take to help solve it.

Let me turn first to where we now stand.

The Population Background

Last year the world's total population passed the four billion mark. On the face of it, the event was not very dramatic. It marked, of course, the largest number of human beings ever to have been alive simultaneously on the planet—and thus was a record of sorts. But that particular record is broken every year. And will continue to be broken every year long beyond the lifespan of anyone alive today.

Barring a holocaust brought on by man or nature, the world's population today is the smallest it will ever be again.

How did it reach a population of four billion? For the first 99 percent of man's existence, surprisingly slowly. For the last one percent of his history, in a great rush.

Table 1
The Rate of Growth of the World's Population

Year	Total Population	Rate of Growth Per Year Since Previous Date	Doubling Time
1,000,000 B.C.	a few thousand	—	—
8,000 B.C.	8 million	0.0007%	100,000 years
1 A.D.	300 million	0.046	1,500
1750	800 million	0.06	1,200
1900	1,650 million	0.48	150
1970	3,600 million	1.0	70
2000	6,300 million	2.0	35

Man has been on earth for a million years or more. For most of those millenia, his life was largely a search for a secure food supply. During the period that he was without pastoral or agricultural technology, adequate tools, or much protection against a harsh environment, he had a birth rate that only barely kept pace with the death rate.

As a consequence, until the dawn of agriculture around 8000 B.C., the population, after ten thousand centuries, had reached only an estimated eight million. During this immense interval, the average annual rate of increase was only about one additional individual for every 150,000 persons.

With the advent of agriculture and the domestication of animals, the food supply became more dependable, and the eight million population of 8000 B.C. rose to about 300 million by the beginning of the Christian era. This meant an average annual rate of increase of 65 persons for every 150,000—or as demographers would express it today, a growth rate of .046 percent.

From A.D. 1 to the middle of the eighteenth century, the population ebbed and flowed, gaining in prosperous periods, and falling back sharply in times of trouble. The bubonic plague—the Black Death—struck Europe suddenly in the mid-fourteenth century, and in four years cut down one person in every three. By the year 1400, under the onslaught of further epidemics, the European population had fallen to little more than half what it had been only fifty years earlier.

Thus by 1750, the total had reached only about 800 million. Then, as the industrial revolution gathered momentum, population growth began rapidly to accelerate. By 1900 it had doubled to 1.6 billion; by 1964 it had doubled again to 3.2 billion; and by the end of the century it is projected to double again to about 6.3 billion.

Now these numbers—as abstract as they may seem—illustrate an important point about population dynamics. The doubling time is extremely sensitive to very minor increments in the average annual growth rate.

It took mankind more than a million years to reach a population of one billion. But the second billion required only 120 years; the third billion 32 years; and the fourth billion 15 years. If one postulates that the human race began with a single pair of parents, the population has had to double only 31 times to reach its present huge total.

At the current global growth rate of about 2 percent, the world's population will add a fifth billion in about 11 years. But these global totals, of course, obscure wide demographic differences between the developed and developing countries.

During the period from 1750 to 1850, the two groups of countries grew at similar average annual rates: .6 percent for the developed, .4 percent for the developing. From 1850 to 1950, the rates were .9 percent and .6 percent. From 1950 to 1975 the rates changed dramatically and became, respectively, 1.1 percent and 2.2 percent. The recent growth rates in the developing countries are not only twice as great as those in the developed countries today, but exceed by an equally large margin the most rapid growth ever experienced by the developed countries.

Translating these growth trends, and relative population sizes, into absolute numbers of people demonstrates the historical pattern even more graphically. From 1750 to 1850 the developed countries grew annually by 1.5 million people and the developing countries by 3 million; from 1850 to 1950, by 5 million and 7 million respectively; and from 1950 to 1975, by 11 million, and 48 million.

Demographic Dynamics*

To grasp fully what is happening here, it is helpful to recall the fundamental dynamics of population increase. On the surface they seem simple enough: population growth for any given society is the excess of births over deaths, as modified by migration.

If we disregard, for the moment, the influence of migration, it is apparent that so-called stationary, or steady-state, populations are those in which births and deaths are in balance. For thousands of centuries the world had something very close to just that.

To achieve a steady-state population there must be a stable age structure and replacement-level fertility: a child must be born to replace each person in the parent generation. That seems obvious enough, but since some

*At the end of this chapter is a glossary that defines several terms used in analyzing demographic dynamics.

females die before or during childbearing age, the average number of children that parents in a given society must have to keep the population stationary is a function of the mortality conditions in the society.

In the Ivory Coast, for example, the death rates in the late 1960s of potential childbearing women were such that 3.5 births per woman would have been required to replace the parent generation; whereas in the United States, where death rates were much lower, only 2.1 births per woman were needed. In actuality, of course, fertility in the Ivory Coast, as in almost all of Africa, is much higher than that; and fertility in the United States has, since 1972, been below the replacement level.

Replacement is measured by the net reproduction rate (NRR), which technically refers to the number of daughters born per woman who could survive to childbearing age, assuming the prevailing levels of fertility and mortality. An NRR of 1.0 is the exact replacement level, and means that on average each woman would have one daughter who could be expected to live to the mean age of reproduction.

When female death rates prior to the end of the reproductive age are high, it clearly requires greater total fertility per woman to maintain a stationary population. When such death rates fall, it requires proportionately less. We know, too, what are the outer limits of the various female mortality-fertility combinations that can produce a stationary population.

Today in the developed countries over 95% of women survive through childbearing years. Under such conditions, a total fertility rate of only 2.1 children per woman suffices for replacement. On the other hand, average female life expectancy of 15 is the highest feasible mortality rate any large population could sustain, since in such a case only about 25 percent of women live to have children, and they would have to have an average of almost 9 children apiece to keep the population from declining. While it is, of course, physiologically possible for individual women to give birth to more than that number, no large grouping has ever been observed with a total fertility rate much higher than 8 to 9 births per woman.

This explains how near zero growth prevailed in the world's population for thousands of centuries. Life expectancy at birth was very low, probably about 20 years. This meant that only about a third of the females born survived to the mean age of childbearing, and that those who lived to the age of menopause had an average of about 6.5 children; a birth rate of 50 to 55 per 1,000.

Even as late as the eighteenth century, mortality in Europe remained very high. In France, for example, almost a quarter of the population died before they reached their first birthday, and nearly half before the age of 20. By the early 1960s, only 2 percent died in their first year, and only 4 percent died before reaching 20. It is these low mortality rates that permit population levels to be maintained with only 2.1 children per female (a crude birth rate of roughly 14 per 1,000). In actual fact, women through-out the developed world today have an average number of children ranging from less than 2 to about 3.

Developing countries today typically have a female life expectancy at birth of about 55; total fertility rates averaging about 5.3 children per woman; and crude birth rates of about 37 per 1,000.[1] This combination results in a growth rate of approximately 2.3 percent, doubling the popula-tion every 30 years. To reach replacement-level fertility, at current mor-tality rates, would require a reduction in the total fertility rate to 2.6, and the crude birth rate to about 20 per 1,000.

But when a net reproduction rate of 1.0—replacement-level fertility—is reached in a society, it does not mean that the population immediately ceases to grow. It will continue increasing for decades. That is a function of the society's age structure.

The population will continue to grow because the higher birth rates of the past have produced an age distribution with a relatively high propor-tion of persons currently in, or still to enter, the reproductive ages. This in turn will result in more births than deaths until the population changes to the older age distribution intrinsic in the low birth rate. Thus, even at re-placement-level fertility, the population does not become stationary until the age structure stabilizes, which takes 60 to 70 years.

The difference in age distribution between a society that is in a period

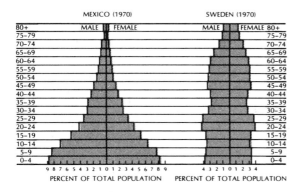

Figure 2 Comparison of Mexican and Swedish age distributions

of high birth rates and falling death rates, and one that has been experiencing low birth rates and low death rates for many years, can be seen by comparing the population profiles of Mexico and Sweden (Figure 2).

Because of Mexico's very young age distribution, even after that country reaches and maintains replacement levels of fertility,[2] approximately seventy additional years will pass before its age profile will approximate the Swedish pattern. During that entire seventy-year period, Mexico's population will continue to increase. Mexico's case is typical of the developing countries. And therefore the time lag of something like seventy years applies to that entire group of countries. But the seventy-year countdown cannot even begin, of course, until the replacement level of fertility is actually reached.

And here we come to a point of immense importance—one that is not well understood, and one that I want strongly to emphasize: the speed at which fertility in the world declines to the replacement level will have a very significant effect on the ultimate size of the stationary population. For every decade of delay in achieving a net reproduction rate of 1.0—replacement level—the world's ultimate steady-state population will be about 15 percent greater.

The significance of this statement can be understood by applying it to the present outlook. If current trends in fertility rates continue, that is, if crude birth rates in developing countries decline by approximately 6 points per decade, it appears that the world might reach a net reproduction rate of 1.0 in about the year 2020. This would lead to a steady-state population of 11 billion some 70 years later.

If the date at which replacement-level fertility is reached could be advanced from 2020 to 2000 (by following, for example, the suggestions made later in this paper), the ultimate population would be approximately 3 billion less, a number equivalent to 75 percent of today's world total. This reveals in startling terms the hidden penalties of failing to act, and act immediately, to reduce fertility.

If global replacement levels of fertility were to be reached around the year 2000, with the world ultimately stabilizing at about 8 billion, 90 percent of the increase over today's levels would be in the developing countries. As shown in the table below it would mean, if each country followed the same general pattern, an India of 1.4 billion; a Brazil of 275 million; a Bangladesh of 245 million; a Nigeria of 200 million; and a Mexico of 175 million.

But as I have pointed out, given today's level of complacency in some quarters, and discouragement in others, the more likely scenario is a world

Table 2
The Ultimate Size of Stationary Population in Selected Developing Countries
(in millions)

Country	Pop. 1975	Ultimate Stationary Population[a]		
		NRR of 1.0 Achieved in Year 2000	NRR of 1.0 Achieved in Year 2020	% Increase Caused by Two Decades of Delay
India	620	1,400	2,000	43
Brazil	110	275	390	42
Bangladesh	76	245	400	63
Nigeria	65	200	320	60
Mexico	62	175	270	54

Source: Frejka, Tomas, *The Future of Population Growth; Alternative Paths to Equilibrium,* Population Council, New York, 1973.

[a]The Stationary Population level will be reached about 70 years after the date on which a NRR of 1.0 is realized.

stabilized at about 11 billion. Populations in the developing countries would be 40 to 60 percent greater than indicated above because of two decades of delay in reaching replacement levels of fertility.

We have to try to comprehend what such a world would really be. We call it stabilized, but what kind of stability would be possible? Can we assume that the levels of poverty, hunger, stress, crowding, and frustration that such a situation could cause in the developing nations—which by then would contain nine out of every ten human beings on earth—would be likely to assure social stability? Or political stability? Or, for that matter, military stability? It is not a world that anyone wants.

Even in our present world of 4 billion, excessive population growth severely penalizes many of the developing nations.[3] It drains away resources, dilutes per capita income, and widens inequalities. At the national level, the government must devote more and more investment simply to provide minimal services to an ever-increasing number of children. At the family level, the same needs press in on the parents of large families.

During their early years, most children are primarily consumers rather than producers. For both the government and the family, more children mean more expenditure on food, on shelter, on clothing, on health, on education, on every essential social service. And it means correspondingly less expenditure on investment to achieve the very economic growth required to finance these services.

As children reach adulthood, the problem is compounded by mounting unemployment. There are not enough jobs to go round because the government—grappling with the daily demands of the increasing numbers—

has been unable to invest enough in job-producing enterprises. Thus the cycle of poverty and overpopulation tightens—each reinforcing the other—and the entire social and economic framework weakens under the weight of too great a dependency ratio.[4]

The sudden global surge in population over the past quarter-century has, of course, been a function of two opposite trends: the gradual slowing down of the growth rate in the developed nations, and the rapid acceleration of the growth rate in the developing countries. The experience of the developed countries gave rise to the theory of the demographic transition.

The Demographic Transition
The theory holds that societies tend to move through three distinct demographic stages:

1. high birth rates, and high death rates, resulting in near stationary populations;
2. high birth rates, but declining death rates, producing growing populations;
3. and finally, low birth rates and low death rates, reestablishing near stationary populations.

If one examines the history of the developed nations, the facts support the theory. Preindustrial societies grew very slowly. Birth rates and death rates generally were both high, and very nearly in balance. But with the advent of industrialization, more adequate nutrition, and improved public health measures, death rates gradually began to fall, and growth rates to increase.

The process continued in the industrializing societies into our own century until birth rates in turn began to diminish, and growth to level off.[5] Today in all but two or three developed countries fertility rates are near, or at—and in some cases even below—replacement levels. As a consequence, in 1975, the total fertility rate for the developed countries as a group was 2.1, exactly at replacement level. It has taken the developed world as a whole about 150 years to pass through the demographic transition.

But most of the developing countries remain today in the second stage of the transition. Their birth rates range between 30 and 50 per thousand, and their death rates between 10 and 25 per thousand. The result is that as a group their population is growing at about 2.3 percent, and at that pace it will double in about 30 years.

Now, if the developing countries were to require 150 years to complete the transition, the world's population would grow from its present 4 billion not to 8 or 11, but to 15 or 16 billion. No one believes it will actually reach that magnitude. But no one is very certain what precisely is going to avert it, short of a major catastrophe brought on by human folly, or by nature's revenge.

The fundamental question is: what, if anything, can rationally and humanely be done to accelerate the demographic transition in the developing world? Some serious observers say nothing can be done. I do not share that view. And to explain why I do not, I want to turn now to a more detailed examination of the current demographic situation in the developing countries.

Recent Demographic Trends

One, as always, must begin with the most recent data. And one, as always, must begin with cautions about the data. They are preliminary, and they are not very precise, and they are at best only suggestive of trends. But the trend they suggest is cautiously encouraging.

What appears to have happened in the developing world over the six-year period, 1969–1975 (see Table 3) is that the crude birth rate (CBR)—the number of births per thousand of population—has declined 3.9 points. The crude death rate (CDR)—the number of deaths per thousand—during the same period has declined 1.9 points. The result is that the rate of natural increase (NI) declined slightly.

If we expand the six-year period to a two-decade period, 1955–1974, as in Table 4, the birth rates appear to have declined an average of about 5.6 points in 20 years, or nearly 13 percent. By major region, the decline has

Table 3
Birth Rates and Death Rates in Developing and Developed Countries

	Developing Countries[a]			Developed Countries			Total World[b]		
	Crude Birth Rate	Crude Death Rate	Rate of Natural Increase	Crude Birth Rate	Crude Death Rate	Rate of Natural Increase	Crude Birth Rate	Crude Death Rate	Rate of Natural Increase
1969	42.9	17.0	2.6	18.0	9.1	0.9	32.0	13.3	1.9
1975	39.0	15.1	2.4	17.3	9.3	0.8	30.0	12.3	1.8

Source: United Nations, *Selected World Demographic Indicators by Countries, 1950-2000*, May 1975; and Population Council Data Bank.

[a]Excludes People's Republic of China (PRC).

[b]Includes rough estimates of data relating to PRC.

Robert S. McNamara 128

Table 4
Crude Birth Rate Trends in Developing and Developed Countries

Region	No. of Countries	1975 Pop. (Millions)	Crude Birth Rates (per thousand)				
			1955	1960	1965	1970	1974
Africa	38	366	48.5	48.3	47.9	47.1	46.2
Latin America	21	289	43.0	42.2	40.8	39.4	37.6
Asia[a]	34	1,318	44.6	44.8	43.5	41.9	38.1
Total: LDC[a]	93	1,973	45.1	45.1	44.1	42.4	39.5
Total: DC	35	1,124	22.3	21.3	18.9	17.3	16.6

Source: UN data as revised by Parker Mauldin of the Population Council.
[a]Excludes People's Republic of China (PRC).

Table 5
Trends in the Percentage Decline in Crude Birth Rates in Developing Countries

	1955–60	1960–65	1965–70	1970–74
Africa	0.4	0.8	1.7	1.9
Latin America	1.9	3.3	3.4	4.6
Asia[a]	−0.4	2.9	3.7	9.1
Total[a]	0.0	2.2	3.9	6.8

Source: UN data revised by Parker Mauldin of the Population Council.
[a]Excludes People's Republic of China.

been 6.5 points in Asia; 5.4 points in Latin America; and 2.3 points in Africa. Further, this decline of the CBR was general and widespread. It occurred in 77 of the 88 developing countries for which estimates are available. Significantly, the decline appears to be gathering momentum: in the developing countries it is less for the earlier years, and greater for the more recent years as shown in Table 5.

But even if the higher rates of decline were to continue into the future, it would mean only six points off the CBR in a decade. And that is only about half of the generally accepted target of one point a year. Thus, though the trend in birth rates is encouraging, its pace is still far too slow. Moreover, the overall CBR decline obscures wide variations among individual countries as shown in Table 6.

Among those nations with populations of more than 50 million, India achieved the greatest CBR reduction, possibly as much as 17 percent; and Indonesia the second best, possibly 13 percent. Bangladesh, on the other hand, and Nigeria, registered no decline at all.

In countries with populations of 20 to 50 million, several demonstrated very large reductions: Korea, 30 percent; and Thailand, Turkey, Colombia, and Egypt, 25 percent each. But the Philippines, Iran, Burma, Zaire, and

Table 6

Reductions in the Crude Birth Rate in Selected Developing Countries: 1955–1974

Country	1975 Pop. (in millions)	% Decrease in CBR	CBR in 1974
Group I (over 50 million)			
India	598	17	36
Indonesia	132	13	42
Mexico	60	11	40
Brazil	108	7	39
Pakistan	70	5	47
Bangladesh	79	0	47
Nigeria	63	0	50
Group II (20 to 50 million)			
South Korea	35	30	28
Thailand	42	25	37
Turkey	39	25	33
Colombia	25	25	32
Egypt	37	25	35
Burma	31	5	40
Philippines	42	5	36
Iran	34	5	43
Zaire	25	5	45
Ethiopia	28	5	48
Group III (under 20 million)			
Africa:			
Mauritius	0.9	37	25
Tunisia	5.6	21	36
Americas:			
Costa Rica	2.0	42	30
Barbados	0.2	35	21
Chile	10.3	33	23
Trinidad & Tobago	1.1	30	24
Panama	1.7	24	31
Asia:			
Singapore	2.3	55	18
Taiwan	16.0	47	23
Hong Kong	4.4	44	18
Fiji	0.6	37	28
Sri Lanka	13.6	27	27
Malaysia	10.5	27	30

Source: The Population Council, *Population and Family Planning Programs: A Fact-book, 1976.* UN data on birth rates revised by Parker Mauldin of the Population Council.

Ethiopia—all countries with very high birth rates—showed only slight declines of less than 5 percent.

Finally, among the smaller developing countries, the CBR went down by more than 40 percent in two, and by more than 20 percent in all the others listed in Table 6. Most of the larger declines occurred in the last decade, again suggesting the existence of a genuine trend, rather than merely an insignificant statistical aberration.

But, I emphasize, statistics in this field are fragmentary, and the situation they describe varies widely from country to country.

It is, then, too soon to be fully certain, but the indications do suggest that crude birth rates in the developing world—outside sub-Saharan Africa —have at last begun to turn downward. Now, if this conclusion is confirmed by the various censuses scheduled for 1980, then what we are witnessing here is a historic change of immense moment. Its importance lies in this. Experience illustrates that once fertility turns definitely downward from high levels, it generally does not reverse direction until it has fallen quite low. Further, the higher the level at which it starts down, the more rapid is its descent.

All of this is obviously a welcome development—if it is in fact taking place. And a reasonable interpretation of the admittedly incomplete data indicates that it is. It is welcome particularly because it is far easier to expedite a declining fertility trend once it has really begun, than it is to initiate it in the first place. But it is essential that we remain realistic. The truth is that at best the current rate of decline in fertility in the developing countries is neither large enough, nor rapid enough, to avoid their ultimately arriving at steady-state populations far in excess of more desirable—and attainable—levels. And I repeat: for every decade of delay in achieving a net reproduction rate of 1.0—replacement-level fertility—the world's ultimate steady-state population will be approximately 15 percent greater.[6]

Current trends, as I have noted, point to a finally stabilized global population of about 11 billion. If we accelerate those trends sufficiently to save two decades of time, it would reduce that dangerous pressure on the planet by approximately 3 billion: 75 percent of the world's current total. Is that acceleration realistically possible? It is. How, then, can we achieve it?

Let me turn to that subject now, and begin by examining the causes and determinants of fertility decline.

Causes and Determinants of Fertility Decline

The task of understanding the factors leading to fertility decline is difficult. The complexities greatly outweigh the certainties. But it is at least possible to draw a number of tentative conclusions from recent research.

We can start with the basic fact that the demographic transition in the industrialized countries demonstrates that socioeconomic development and mortality declines were accompanied by significant reductions in fertility.

That is clear enough. But what is not clear is this: which of the many elements of general development led to that specific result, and with what relative effectiveness? Must the developing countries reach the current levels of income per capita in the developed nations before they reach their fertility rates?

The question is further complicated by the evidence that certain culturally similar regions—those, for example, with a common language or ethnic background—moved through the fertility transition at the same pace, even though their economic conditions differed substantially. This suggests that in these instances cultural considerations were more decisive than economic advance. Further, there is ample evidence that vastly different fertility rates exist in developing countries with the same income levels, and that rates of change in fertility rates appear to bear little correlation with changes in income per capita.

The truth appears to be that a complicated mix of variables is at work, some economic, some not. Mortality decline, urbanization, educational advance, higher aspirations for one's self and one's children—all these elements appear to be involved in differing combinations.

Though we can learn from the experience of the developed nations, we must recognize that their historical circumstances were quite dissimilar to those in the developing countries today. The developed nations entered their fertility transition with lower birth rates, lower growth rates, and much more gradual mortality declines. By the time their death rates had fallen substantially, their industrial infrastructure was already in place. Expanding job opportunities were available either in the cities, or in the New World overseas, which received tens of millions of European immigrants. Further, the age of marriage was relatively late, and the literacy rate relatively high.

The developing nations are confronted with a very different set of circumstances, some of them unfavorable, but some of them advantageous.

Their mortality decline has been the most precipitous in history: five times faster than in the developed nations. In the eight years between 1945 and 1953, Sri Lanka, for example, had as great a decline in mortality as had occurred in Sweden in the entire century between 1771 and 1871. That phenomenon has rapidly driven up growth rates all over the developing world. On the other hand, both individual families and government policy-makers can directly perceive that the number of surviving children is much greater than in the recent past, and this may well move them to consider a smaller family norm.

Compared to the last century, the means of controlling birth are far more numerous, more effective, and more easily available. Modern mass communications are both more pervasive, and more influential. The elite in the developing countries, and increasingly the mass of the people as well, are becoming more aware of living standards in the developed world, including smaller family size and less traditional life styles. Exposure to alternate possibilities stirs their imaginations, and affects their aspirations. Governments have much greater ability now to reach across subnational barriers of linguistic, ethnic, and cultural differences, and can stay in touch with villagers, if they choose to do so. Debate about education policy continues, but most developing countries regard basic literacy for both males and females as essential for development goals, and greater national unity.

Finally, there are an increasing number of governments in the developing world committed to lowering fertility, and an even larger number supporting family planning programs. In 1969, when as President of the World Bank I spoke on population, at the University of Notre Dame, only about 40 developing countries officially supported family planning, and only 20 of those had specific policies to reduce fertility. By 1975 there were 63 countries with official family planning programs, and 34 with explicit policies to reduce the growth rate.[7]

Now all of this is encouraging. And in view of it, what are the conclusions we can draw about the linkages between socioeconomic development and fertility? More specifically, which are those key elements that can be deliberately managed so as to accelerate fertility reduction?

Linkage of Fertility Decline to Social and Economic Development
We still cannot be as certain as we would like in this matter, but we do know that the following factors are important:

Health: Improving the level of health, particularly of children, insures the survival of a desired minimum of offspring, and provides parents with greater incentive for planning and investment for both their children and themselves. Since 1950, all substantial fertility declines in the developing countries have been preceded by substantial declines in mortality.

Education: Broadening the knowledge of both males and females beyond their familiar and local milieu enables them to learn about and take advantage of new opportunities, and to perceive the future as something worth planning for, including personal family size.

Broadly Distributed Economic Growth: Tangible improvement in the living standards of a significant proportion of the low-income groups in a society provides visible proof that aspirations for a better life can in fact be realized, and that a more compact family size can have economic advantages.

Urbanization: Despite the many problems connected with migration from the countryside to the city, it generally does offer greater accessibility to health services and education; increased familiarity with the more modern economic sector; and new savings and consumption patterns: all of which tends to alter attitudes towards traditional family size.

Enhanced Status of Women: Expanding the social, political, occupational, and economic opportunities of women beyond the traditional roles of motherhood and housekeeping enables them to experience directly the advantages of lowered fertility, and to channel their creative abilities over a much broader spectrum of choice.

Now let me sum up here what we have been discussing. The central issue is: which are those specific elements of economic and social development that bear most effectively on reducing fertility? I have suggested several. But how can we be sure they are likely to work? One way is to examine carefully the available data for any apparent correlations with indicated levels of the crude birth rates.

The data demonstrate that there are such apparent correlations. What they do not prove conclusively is an ironclad causal connection. But the figures in Table 7 and those in Table 8 do establish that fertility levels and levels of certain specific socioeconomic indices tend to move together.

Thus declining levels of infant mortality, and rising levels of nutrition, literacy, and nonagricultural employment appear to be accompanied by lower birth rates. In 1970, for example, countries with a crude birth rate greater than 45, had on average an infant mortality rate of 128 per 1,000; an adult literacy rate of 33 percent; and 77 percent of the male labor force in agriculture. Countries with a crude birth rate about 5 points less—

Table 7

"Correspondence" in 1970 between Crude Birth Rates and Selected Development
Indicators[a]

	No. of Countries	CBR Over 45	CBR 40 to 44	CBR 30 to 39	CBR Less Than 30
Health Infant mortality (rate per thousand)	34	128	84	61	20
Life expectancy (years)	43	46	57	64	68
Education Literacy (percent of population over 15 years of age)	39	33	57	78	80
Urbanization Adult male labor in agriculture (percent of total male labor)	46	77	64	45	15

Source: Population Council Data Bank.

[a]The values shown for the development indicators at each level of CBR are median
values for the countries in the sample.

Table 8

Trends of Crude Birth Rates and Selected Development Indicators: 1960–1970

	Number of Countries[a]	Median Value of CBR and Devel. Indicators		Percentage Change
		1960	1970	
Crude birth rate	26	46	42	− 9%
Health Crude death rate (per thousand)	22	11.8	9.8	−17
Life expectancy (years)	17	57	61.4	+ 8
Infant mortality rate (per thousand)	15	80	68	−15
Inhabitants per physician	46	7,730	6,212	−20
Nutrition Calorie consumption (per capita per day)	34	2,110	2,310	+ 9
Protein consumption (grams per capita per day)	33	55.9	61.3	+10
Education Literate as % of population (age 15 and over)	14	61	74	+21
Urbanization Adult male labor in agriculture (%)	24	60	54	−11

[a]All developing countries for which data are available for both 1960 and 1970. The
data are derived from the data banks of the UN Research Institute for Social Development.

a CBR of 40 to 44—had on average an infant mortality rate of 84: a literacy rate of 57 percent; and 64 percent of the male labor force in agriculture. But for countries with CBRs in the range of 30 to 39, infant mortality on average had fallen to 61; literacy had climbed to 78 percent and
only 45 percent of the male labor force was in agriculture. Finally, for
countries with crude birth rates of less than 30, the infant mortality rate
on average was down to 20; literacy was at 80 percent; and only 15 percent of the male labor force was in agriculture.

The correspondence in these examples is clear. The higher levels of
health and education and nonagricultural employment are associated with
lower levels of fertility. But I want to repeat again: the correlation appears
to be with specific elements of development—literacy, for example, and
nutrition and infant mortality—rather than with the general level of economic wealth.

Consider the examples of Korea and Mexico. Both countries have
achieved impressive gains in their gross national products: Mexico since
1940, and Korea since the early 1960s. But by 1973, Mexico had reached
a GNP per capita of $890, whereas Korea stood at less than half of that, at
about $400. Korea, however, had managed to distribute that much smaller
income much more evenly than Mexico. In 1969, the poorest 40 percent
of the households in Korea received 21.4 percent of total income, whereas
the same group in Mexico received only 10.2 percent.

·The infant mortality rate in Korea was at a considerably lower level: in
1970 it was 38, compared to 61 in Mexico. Adult literacy, in the same
year, was greater in Korea: 91 percent versus 84 percent in Mexico. And
by 1970, Korea had decisively entered her fertility transition with a crude
birth rate of 29; whereas Mexico, with a CBR of 45, had not. This, then,
was a case of substantially higher overall national income failing to corr-
relate with either fertility reduction, or other socially desirable factors.

A similar example is the state of Kerala in India. In terms of average per
capita income, it is one of the poorer Indian states. But its distribution of
income is more equal; its literacy rate, particularly for women, is the
highest in the country; and its infant mortality rate is the lowest. In 1974
its crude birth rate was 28, lower than that of any other Indian state.

What these cases, and others, indicate is that gains in overall national
economic growth are most related to fertility declines when they are associated with a broad distribution of the fundamental elements of social
advance. A study of 40 developing countries revealed that an increase of
$10 in the income of the lower 60 percent of the income strata, carrying
with it advances in nutrition, health, and literacy, was associated with a

crude birth rate decline of 0.7 per 1,000; but that a $10 increase in the overall average income of everyone was associated with a CBR decline of only 0.3 per 1,000.

If the growth in national income does not result in improvements of the living conditions of the lower income groups, it will not help to reduce fertility throughout the society.

Extrapolating the Data

The correlation, then, in developing countries between certain social changes and fertility reductions is persuasive, and is supported by the trends from 1960 to 1970. During that decade, literacy and education advanced; infant mortality declined; life expectancy increased; and the crude birth rate fell. Assuming that the social indicators continue to change at the rate of that decade, and that their relation to fertility patterns remains the same, the crude birth rate in the developing countries as a whole would drop approximately half a point per year.

What this means is that without additional intervention, the current population in the developing world is going to continue to grow at rates very substantially in excess of those that would facilitate far more economic and social progress. It is these rates which would lead to an ultimate steady-state population in the world of 11 billion. That is clearly undesirable. Governments, then, must intervene. But how precisely? Let us examine the choices available.

Possible Interventions to Reduce Fertility

The range of possible interventions divides into two broad categories:

those designed to encourage couples to desire smaller families;

and those designed to provide parents with the means to implement that desire.

Both approaches are, of course, necessary. The first sets out to alter the social and economic environment that tends to promote high fertility, and by altering it to create among parents a new and smaller norm of family size, and therefore a demand for birth control. And the second supplies the requisite means that will make that new norm attainable.

Thus family planning services are essential, but in the end can succeed only to the extent that a demand for lower fertility exists. That demand apparently does not now exist in sufficient strength in most of the developing countries.

There are a number of policy actions that governments can take to help stimulate the demand. None of them is easy to implement. All of them require some reallocation of scarce resources. And some of them are politically sensitive. But governments must measure those costs against the immeasurably greater costs in store for societies that procrastinate while dangerous population pressures mount.

What, then, are those specific social and economic actions most likely to promote the desire for reduced fertility? Governments should try to:

Reduce current infant and child mortality rates sharply.

Expand basic education and increase the proportion of girls in school.

Increase the productivity of smallholders in the rural areas, and expand earning opportunities in the cities for low-income groups.

Put greater stress on more equitable distribution of income and services in the drive for greater economic growth.

And above all else, raise the status of women socially, economically, and politically.

Let me comment briefly on each of these.

Reducing Infant and Child Mortality

We know from the experience of both the developed and developing countries that a decline in fertility rates can be expected to follow a reduction in infant and child mortality. The current rates in the developing world remain up to 20 times higher than they are in the developed nations.

Over half of all the deaths in Egypt, for example, occur before the age of five. Comparable and even higher rates are common in other developing countries. In Mexico, Cameroon, and Colombia about 30 percent of all deaths occur in the first year, and 15 to 20 percent of all deaths in the second through the fourth year. In contrast, in Sweden, the United States, and Japan the deaths of infants and children below the age of 5 make up less than 5 percent of the total number. Average rates of infant mortality—deaths per 1,000 in the first year—are 142 in Africa, 121 in Asia, and 60 in Latin America. In the developed countries they average about 20.

Why are they so high in the developing world? Largely because of low nutritional standards, poor hygienic conditions, and inadequate health services. In most developing countries health expenditures have been excessively devoted to supplying a small urban elite with expensive curative health-care systems—highly skilled doctors and elaborate hospitals—that fail to reach 90 percent of the people. What are required are less sophis-

ticated, but more effective, preventive health delivery systems that reach
the mass of the population.

Even quite poor countries can succeed in this, provided sound policies
are pursued. Some 20 years ago, for example, Sri Lanka decided to improve rural health facilities. The result over the past two decades has been
a decline in infant mortality from 78 per 1,000 to 45 per 1,000, an increase in life expectancy from 56 to 69 years, and an associated decline
in the crude birth rate from 39 to 29.

Korea has followed a similar policy, with similar results. But many other
countries—countries even with a much higher per capita national income
than either Sri Lanka or Korea—have spent as much or more on health,
and by failing to stress simple, inexpensive, but effective rural health systems, have reaped much poorer results.

Turkey, for example, had a GNP per capita of $860 in 1975, compared
to Korea's $550 and Sri Lanka's $150, but has concentrated on urban
health, with conventional facilities, and today has an infant mortality
rate of 119 per 1,000, as compared to Korea's 38 per 1,000; life expectancy of 60 years, compared with Korea's 64 years; and a crude birth rate
of 39, as compared with Korea's 28.

Infant and child mortality rates can be brought down relatively simply
and inexpensively, if the national health policies are carefully designed.
The return in lowered fertility, and healthier children, and more equitably
served families is clearly worth the effort.

Expanding Basic Education

Education, like health, has often been a casualty of inappropriate policies,
and there is wide debate over what ought best to be done. But there is no
question that expanding the educational opportunities of females cor-
relates with lowered fertility. In Latin America, for example, studies indicate that in districts as diverse as Rio de Janeiro, rural Chile, and Buenos
Aires, women who have completed primary school average about two children fewer than those who have not. Schooling tends to delay the age of
marriage for girls, and thus reduces their total possible number of childbearing years.

Further, education facilitates, for both men and women, the acquisi-
tion of information on family planning. It increases their exposure to mass
media and printed material, and enables them to learn about modern contraceptives and their use.

Schooling, too, clearly enhances a girl's prospects of finding employment
outside the home that may compete with raising a large family. In a com-

parative study of 49 countries, the level of female education in each nation demonstrated a significant impact on the proportion of women earning wages or salaries, which in turn had a strong association with lowered fertility.

While children are in school, they do not contribute much to the support of the family, and thus parents tend to perceive them as having less immediate economic utility, but more long-term earning capacity. Both these factors are likely to lead parents toward a more compact family norm, since a large family is more expensive to educate, and a small, well-educated one will be in a better position to aid parents in later life. Fertility rates are substantially higher in those countries in which children under 15 are economically active, rather than in school. Parents with an education themselves typically desire an even better education for their children, and realize that if these aspirations are to be achieved, family size will have to be limited.

Education leads to lowered fertility, too, by reducing infant and child mortality. In Northeast Brazil one of the chief motivations for school attendance was found to be the nutritious school lunch program. Further, a parent who has had some schooling is likely to be more careful about basic sanitation, and the value of innoculations and antibiotics. Such a mother is more confident that her own children will survive, and is less likely to want additional children merely as insurance against some dying.

Finally, perhaps the greatest benefit of education to both men and women in heavily traditional environments is that it broadens their view of the opportunities and potential of life, inclines them to think more for themselves, and reduces their suspicion of social change. This creates an intellectual environment in which important questions such as family size and contraceptive practice can be discussed more openly.

There is little likelihood that governments in developing countries—or for that matter, in developed countries—will soon agree over the competing strategies for more effective school systems. But one principle is beyond dispute: in the face of perennial budgetary pressures, it is far better to try to provide a basic minimum of practical and development-oriented education for many, than to opt for an expensive, formal, and overly academic education for a few.

A basic learning package, for both men and women, including functional literacy and numeracy, some choice of relevant vocational skills for productive activity, family planning and health, child care, nutrition, sanitation, and the knowledge required for active civic participation is an investment no nation can afford not to make. The very nature of the edu-

cational process imposes a relatively long time lag for the economic return on that investment. But if the basic package is right, the return will
be huge. And not the least component of that return will be the benefit
of reduced fertility.

Increasing the Productivity of Small Farmers and Expanding Earning Opportunities in the Cities

As a generality, small farmers in developing countries are among the lowest income groups in the society. Their agricultural productivity is often
at bare subsistence levels. Perhaps the only poorer individuals in the countryside are the landless, whose sole source of income is seasonal on-farm
employment. The fertility of both groups is characteristically high.

Typically the smallholders are reluctant to sell their land, but their
holdings tend to become even smaller and more fragmented as the land
passes through the inheritance process to their surviving sons. The landless are the most likely candidates for migration to the squatter settlements of the city, since they have no tangible assets to hold them in the
rural areas. But, increasingly, the dwindling size of the redivided holdings
forces the inheriting sons as well to sell their uneconomic parcels of land,
and join the procession to the urban slums in search of a job.

For the small farmers who remain on their land their only hope to escape poverty—with its poverty-related fertility levels—is government policy
deliberately designed to assist them to increase their productivity. There is,
in fact, great potential for this, but it requires a comprehensive program of
fundamental elements such as land and tenancy reform; better access to
credit; assured availability of water; expanded extension of facilities;
greater participation in public services; and new forms of rural institutions
that can act as effective intermediaries between the appropriate government ministries and the individual subsistence farmers.

I have discussed in detail the essential components of such a program
elsewhere,[8] and need not repeat them here, except to point out that our
early experience with such rural development projects in the World Bank
confirms their feasibility. We have over the last three years initiated 210
such projects, calculated to at least double the incomes of 8 million farm
families, or about 50 million individuals. It is through this increase in income that such farm families will almost certainly experience a beneficial
decline in their traditionally high fertility. For the income will give them
access to better health and education and living standards, which in turn
are likely to lead to smaller families. There is, then, a sound policy formula

that governments can implement for the poor farmer that both reduces poverty, and its attendant fertility.

But what of the growing millions of poor who migrate to the cities and take their propensity for large families with them? This is a considerably more complex policy problem since urban socioeconomic relationships are by their nature both more varied and more complicated than traditional rural situations. However the basic principle remains the same. Policies must be shaped that will assist the urban poor to increase their productivity. In practice this means a comprehensive program designed to increase earning opportunities in both the traditional and the modern sectors; provide equitable access to public utilities, transport, education, and health services; and establish realistic housing policies.

Again, I have dealt with this subject at length in another context[9] and I need not reiterate the issues here. What is clear is that urbanization has usually been associated with low fertility. In Latin America, for example, studies have indicated that family size in rural areas and small towns is nearly twice as large as those in major urban cities. The correlation has been found in countries as diverse as India, Lebanon, Hungary, the Soviet Union, and Japan.

In the urban setting there are fewer opportunities for children to do useful work, and hence more rationale for them to be in school. In general, cities offer relatively better access to the modern socioeconomic system, and its attendant attitudes. Moreover, migration from the countryside tends to loosen some links with the extended family. If parents cannot expect to dwell with their adult children, there is less incentive for them to have large families for the purpose of support in their old age. Finally, the very act of leaving the traditional family home may lead to other breaks with tradition, such as the age of marriage and family size.

But one must enter a word of caution. From a policy point of view, most governments in the developing world have little practical capacity either to regulate urbanization or to retard it. It simply happens, and it is happening far more rapidly than almost any major city can possibly cope with in an orderly way.

Populations in the countries themselves are doubling every 25 to 30 years, but their large cities are doubling every 10 to 15 years, and the urban slums and shanty towns in these cities every 5 to 7 years. By 1990 Lima, Peru, is expected to have six million inhabitants, 75 percent of whom will live in what were originally squatter settlements.

Fertility may or may not decrease in such potentially huge and squalid surroundings. And if it does decrease, it may decrease for the wrong reasons: inhuman crowding, unbearable stress, or dysfunctional family relationships. What must be countered in exploding cities is the desperate poverty that fuels them, which is itself, in part, the tragic legacy of rampant population growth in the countryside and city alike.

More Equitable Distribution of Economic Growth

While economic growth is a necessary condition of development in a modernizing society, it is not in itself a sufficient condition. The reason is clear. Economic growth cannot change the lives of the mass of people unless it reaches the mass of the people.

It is not doing so with sufficient impact in most of the developing countries of the world today. Typically, the upper 20 percent of the population receives 55 percent of the national income, and the lowest 20 percent receives 5 percent. In the rural areas, this is reflected in the concentration of land ownership. According to an FAO survey, the wealthiest 20 percent of the landowners in most developing countries own between 50 and 60 percent of the cropland. In Venezuela they own 82 percent; in Colombia 56 percent; in Brazil 53 percent; in the Philippines, India, and Pakistan about 50 percent. The roughly 100 million small farms in the developing world—those less than 5 hectares—are concentrated on only 20 percent of the cropland.

What this means is that the lower 40 percent of the income strata is neither contributing significantly to economic growth nor sharing equitably in its benefits. They are the poor, and they are virtually outside the entire development process. It largely passes them by.

It is little wonder, then, that national economic growth in itself has had less than optimum effect on the fertility patterns of the vast mass of the population. Their nations have been progressing, but large numbers of the people have advanced at rates far below the average.

Even the conventional measurements that governments have at hand to trace economic progress can be misleading. The growth of the gross national product, for example, is generally regarded as a key index. And it is, for it measures the total value of the goods and services of the economy. But it does not, and cannot, serve as a measure of their distribution.

Since the upper 40 percent of the population in a developing country typically receives 75 percent of all income, the growth of the GNP is primarily an index of the progress of these upper-income groups. It tells one very little about what is happening to the poorest 40 percent, who collectively receive only about 10 or 15 percent of the total national income.

The implication of much of what was said at the World Population Conference in Bucharest in 1974 was that a sufficient rate of development will
solve any population problem in time. But what precisely is a "sufficient
rate of development"? It clearly is not overall average economic growth,
which so frequently benefits the few and bypasses the many.

Most countries in Latin America, for example, have considerably higher
per capita income than countries in Asia and Africa. And yet fertility rates
are not proportionately lower. That, in part, is a function of the serious
inequalities in income distribution in the Latin American region.

A study of various characteristics in 64 countries from both the developed and developing areas of the world, for which data are available,
confirmed that more equitable income distribution, with the resultant
broader distribution of social service, is strongly associated with lower
fertility. The analysis suggested that each additional percentage point of
total income received by the poorest 40 percent reduces the general fertility rate by about 3 points.

Governments everywhere in the developing world are, of course,
striving to accelerate economic growth. Excessive fertility is itself a serious
obstacle to this growth. But unless the benefits of the growth are directed
more equitably to the lower 40 percent of the income groups, where in
fact fertility rates are likely to be the highest, then economic growth as
such will not move the society forward at an optimum rate of progress.

Enhancing the Status of Women Socially, Economically, and Politically
The importance of enhancing the status of women is critical, and there is a
great deal that governments can do in this matter. In some societies even
simple legislative changes—such as establishing the legal right of a woman
to refuse to marry the mate picked out for her by her parents, or the right
to own property herself—are important first steps in improving her position in society.

Of all the aspects of social development, the educational level appears
most consistently associated with lower fertility. And it is significant that
an increase in the education of women tends to lower fertility to a greater
extent than a similar increase in the education of men. But in most developing societies women do not have equitable access to education. The
number of illiterate females is growing faster than illiterate males. Nearly
two-thirds of the world's 800 million illiterates are women, and virtually
everywhere males are given preference both for general education and
vocational training.

One reason for this is that the prevailing image of women distorts their full contribution to society. Women are esteemed—and are encouraged to esteem themselves—predominantly in their roles as mothers. Their economic contribution, though it is substantial in a number of developing societies, is almost always understated. The fact is that in subsistence societies women generally do at least 50 percent of the work connected with agricultural production and processing, as well as take care of the children, and the housekeeping. They rise earlier and retire later than anyone else in the family, often working 18 hours a day.

But despite this contribution, women generally suffer the most malnutrition in poor families. Men are given first claim on such food as is available; children second; and the mother last. This, in itself, tends to lead to high fertility through a self-perpetuating cycle of events.

Malnourished mothers give birth to weak and unhealthy infants, and have problems nursing them adequately. Such infants often die. This leads to frequent pregnancies. The mothers, constantly pregnant or nursing infants, are unable to play a larger role in the outside-the-home work force. This diminishes their occupational and economic status, which in turn reinforces the concept that males are more important. This makes sons more desirable than daughters. When only daughters are born, another pregnancy must ensue in order to try again for a son. Repeated pregnancy not only increases the family size, but exhausts the mother, weakens her health—and thus the whole cycle begins again.

Though governments sometimes recognize that encouraging women to enter the off-farm and urban work force reduces fertility—since it tends to delay the age of marriage, and increase the interval between children—policymakers are often tempted to conclude that this would only exacerbate unemployment among men, and hence diminish family income. But that objection is a short-term view of the matter. In the longer run, a family with two wage earners, and a smaller number of dependents—due to the related decreased fertility—can contribute more to public revenues through taxes, and more to capital formation through increased savings.

In contrast with a large and poor one-wage-earner family, the smaller two-wage-earner family helps accelerate economic growth, and thus increases the demand for labor, male and female.

The truth is that greater economic opportunity for women and the greater educational opportunity that undergirds it—would substantially reduce fertility. And in societies in which rapid population growth is draining away resources, expenditure on education and training for boys that is not matched by comparable expenditure for girls will very likely be diminished in the end by the girls' continued high fertility. More education for women in developing countries is a very good buy.

Instruction on nutrition, child care, family planning, and home economics are all, of course, important. But women need market-oriented training and services as well: aaccess to credit, extension services, the skills necessary for participating in a cash economy. Schools must make the point to young women that the ideal role of a girl is not be the mother of a large and poor family, but rather to have double role as mother of a small family, and as a wage earner who contributes to the well-being of her family by economic employment.

Women represent a seriously undervalued potential in the development process. And to prolong inequitable practices that relegate them exclusively to narrow traditional roles not only denies both them and society the benefits of that potential, but very seriously compounds the problem of reducing fertility.

Public Information Programs

Those, then, are the specific socioeconomic interventions calculated to encourage smaller families. They must, of course, be paralleled and supported by a continuing public information program.

There is a need to inform, educate, and persuade people of the benefits of a more compact and manageable family size. This is essential, but it has not been an easy task. The significance of the population problem dawned slowly on an unprepared world. There was not only ignorance and skepticism, but in many instances strong opposition against even discussing the subject. That is not surprising. Since reproduction is essential for the survival of a society, it is understandable that every society has had strong views about family size.

Norms in this matter have always existed, and there has always been strong group pressure to see that they were followed. Until very recently, childless women in some societies have been regarded with open scorn. And for males not to father a large family has tended to be a reflection on their masculinity.

Norms are patterns of expected behavior, rules of what is appropriate and what is not. And we know, from surveys on desired family size, what those norms are today in various societies. In the developed world the average desired number of children ranges from 2 to 3. In the developing world the average is between 4 and 6, with a majority wanting at least four children.

This is a critical point, since one of the main objects of intervention in population is to create a set of circumstances in which people will change their norm of desired family size. And there is simply no hope of succeeding at that unless one first clearly understands the reasoning behind their present norms.

To design an effective public information program, to set up a persuasive person-to-person communication scheme, to draft and establish a successful population education plan, it is imperative to comprehend the mind-set that you are attempting to change. And the reasons for fertility reduction that may be persuasive to planners sitting in distant capitals may not be persuasive at all to parents sitting in remote villages.

Village couples rarely worry about the progress of the gross national product. What they may well worry about is the progress of a sick child, or how they are going to accumulate enough savings to secure their old age, and whether the signs are auspicious that the next pregnancy will finally give them a second son, rather than a third daughter.

As we have said, it is the poor, as a generality, who have the most children. And it is the poorest countries, as a generality, that have the highest birth rates. But it is a mistake to think that the poor have children mindlessly, or without purpose, or—in the light of their own personal value systems—irresponsibly. Quite the contrary.

The poor, by the very fact of their poverty, have little margin for error. The very precariousness of their existence habituates them to be cautious. They may be illiterate. They are seldom foolhardy. To survive at all, they are forced to be shrewd.

What we must grasp is that poverty does not make people unreasonable. What it does do is severely reduce their range of choice. They often do what they do because there is little real opportunity to do otherwise. Poor people have large families for many reasons. But the point is they do have reasons. Reasons of security for their old age. Reasons about additional help on the land. Reasons concerning the cultural preference for sons. Reasons related to the laws of inheritance. Reasons dictated by traditional religious behavior. And reasons of personal pride.

Demography measures people. It cannot always measure their inner feelings. And yet understanding poor people—and the narrow range of options that poverty offers them—is the key to assisting them to broaden their choices. In a good public information program, that is precisely what happens. Alternative choices become evident.

The mass media can be helpful, particularly radio, television, and film since they do not depend exclusively on literacy for comprehension. But all the media can be creatively utilized: newspapers, signboards, leaflets, exhibits, village posters, songs, and plays.

Communication research concludes that the mass media, while influential with people who are already in general agreement, or at least neutral, can rarely—through direct messages—persuade people to reverse deep-seated convictions, or long-standing behavior.

However what the media can do, and do very well, is help people to change their views indirectly by putting them in contact with another world, expanding their horizons, stimulating their curiosity, and introducing them to new ideas, including the idea of attractive alternative life styles, with fewer, but more advantaged children.

But in the end, no form of media information is as effective as person-to-person communication. Messages can be sent electronically thousands of miles, but it is ultimately people talking to one another in a classroom, on the street, at the village market, or in the village home where the essential questions are discussed, and the essential answers are explored. Door-to-door field work, discussion groups, study clubs, civic organizations, town and village meetings: all of these are important, and all of them can be made stimulating, informative, and persuasive.

There is a whole spectrum of formal and informal learning situations that can be utilized. Population education as a component of the school curriculum is obvious and essential. Mobile vans visiting villages with films, exhibits, and talks can combine entertainment with instruction. Political leaders, national celebrities, and religious authorities can endorse national population goals in their speeches and public appearances. All of this is possible, given leadership, imagination, and drive. And all of it is very worthwhile.

Beyond these information and educational efforts, there is a whole range of additional measures available to governments that can serve as incentives to postpone the age of marriage, undertake family planning, or adopt new norms of family size and disincentives to retaining inappropriate norms.

Incentives and Disincentives
Housing, and job opportunities, maternity benefits, tax deductions, dependency allowances, pension provisions, school admission priorities: these and similar government benefits and policies can be redesigned to encourage parents to have small families, and to dissuade them from having large ones.

Incentives can range from immediate cash payments to family planning

acceptors to elaborate programs for future payment, at the end of the
childbearing years, for fertility restraint. Disincentives can limit the allocation of various public services on a graduated scale: more to parents with
few children, less—or none at all—to parents with many children.[10]

Incentives, of course, widen rather than restrict choice, and are less
likely to penalize children, who, through no fault of their own, happen to
get born into large families. But the fact is, of course, that disincentives or
not, children born into large families in the developing world today are
likely to be penalized in any case, simply by the pressures of poverty that
the population problem has exacerbated in developing societies.[11] Experimenting with incentives is still relatively limited, but the prospects are
promising. Deferred-payment schemes, which would reward parents finan-
cially at the time of retirement, or at the end of the childbearing age, for
their fertility restraint are particularly worth exploring.

Such schemes attempt to provide parents with an alternative source of
financial security for their old age, in place of the traditional one of large
families. And they encourage the creation of a society in which parents
can put their resources and energies into providing a small number of children with the best possible start in life rather than merely hoping to find
security in a large number of children—each one of whom must face a
proportionately more precarious future.

Promoting a Social Consensus

Governments have considerable capacity, as well, to help create a generalized atmosphere of social consensus in an antinatalist direction. Villages
and local communities, just as individual families, can be rewarded by
government policies for good performance in fertility restraint. Allocations
of central government funds for community improvements—roads, electri-
fication, public works—can be conditioned on evidence of community
commitment to new-style family norms.

India, for example, recently adopted a measure which provides that
both the political representation of local areas, and their allocation of national financial resources, will no longer increase simply as a function of
their population growth. In the future, additional numbers will not automatically mean additional votes or additional claims on tax revenues.

But it is not only the central government in a society that can apply
disincentives to high fertility. Community authorities can do the same. In
preindustrial Japan, for example, a strong tradition of social cooperation
and consensus at the village level maintained severe constraints on the
number of households in the village, often permitting no increase at all.

These social pressures were transmitted to heads of households, who in turn exerted authority over individual household members in matters of marriage, divorce, and adoption. This tradition appears to have been a significant influence in holding population increase during the last 150 years of Tokugawa Japan to less than 0.2 percent a year.

It is obvious that the interest of a local community in the fertility of its membership will be proportional to the social costs of population increase that it is called upon to bear. If schools and other public services are in part locally financed; if pressures on the land lead to local deforestation and erosion; and if local unemployment becomes serious, then communities may well become conscious of the adverse social effects of excessive population growth.

It is clear that there are many different approaches to the task of promoting a new social consensus on population problems within a society, and the choice of one over another—or any particular mix of actions— must, of course, be guided by the cultural context of the society in question. But the truth is that most of the approaches, and all of the actions, are difficult to implement. And we must face the reality that if these approaches fail, and population pressures become too great, nations will be driven to more coercive methods.

Coercion
A number of governments are moving in the direction of coercion already. Some have introduced legal sanctions to raise the age of marriage. A few are considering direct legal limitations on family size, and sanctions to enforce them.

No government really wants to resort to coercion in this matter. But neither can any government afford to let population pressures grow so dangerously large that social frustrations finally erupt into irrational violence and civil disintegration. That would be coercion of a very different order. In effect, it would be nature's response to our own indifference.

Now let me underscore what we have been analyzing here. We have been discussing those kinds of interventions that governments can make to help stimulate the desire among parents for a smaller family size. But those efforts must, of course, be accompanied by corresponding interventions that provide parents with readily available means to do so.

Family Planning Services
Governments must improve the access to the modern means of fertility

control both qualitatively and quantitatively: more and better services to greater numbers of people.

In practice, that requires:

Providing a broad selection of the current contraceptives: pills, condoms, IUDs; as well as sterilization, and—where the society desires it—abortion.

Establishing a broad spectrum of delivery services and informational activities utilizing: physicians in private practice; paramedical workers; professional field workers; community-based local agents; the commercial sector; widespread distribution of contraceptives; sterilization centers; mobile clinics; postpartum arrangements; and the integration of contraceptive services into the maternal and child-health system, the general health system, and the community development system.

And finally, improving the acceptability, continuity, and effectiveness of the means of fertility control by accelerating research on such possibilities as: a contraceptive vaccine; a better implant; an IUD free of side effects; a safer and more convenient pill (a once-a-month pill, or a once-a-year pill); a nonsurgical means to terminate pregnancy; or a currently unknown "ideal" contraceptive.

To put the matter succinctly, governments need to provide a broad choice of present contraceptive techniques and services to parents; they need to improve the delivery system by which parents can get the services they wish; and they need to support continuing research for better techniques and services.

The majority of the world's population lives in countries with family planning programs that now have as their explicit objective the reduction of fertility. And yet the programs themselves often do not reflect much political conviction that they can and must succeed. Many of these programs are small, and rely on foreign sources for much of their finance. All governments, of course, have resource constraints. But fertility reduction, as a priority, seldom commands even one percent of national budgets. Further, governments have often failed to give the programs the status and national attention that would attract top managerial talent. For these, and related reasons, the world's total family planning acceptors did not measurably increase in the period 1972–1975, despite the increase in the number of national programs.

I listed above a number of actions that governments—both developed and developing—can take to strengthen family planning programs. One of the most urgent needs is a much greater effort in reproductive biological research and contraceptive technology.

Reproductive Biological Research
The requirement for a substantial expansion in reproductive research is

obvious. Though by the early 1970s some 46 million women throughout the world were using the IUD or the pill, this did not begin to meet the need. Of the approximately 500 million women around the globe in their childbearing years, and facing the risk of an unwanted pregnancy, an estimated 70 percent are using no contraceptive method at all.

The current estimate is that for the world as a whole, one out of every three or four pregnancies ends in abortion, and the vast majority of the women seeking abortion are married. The fact is that abortion, even though it is still illegal in a number of countries—and remains ethically offensive to millions—appears to be the most widespread means of fertility control there is. That is, in itself, a cogent argument for better contraceptive methods.

Cultural, religious, and personal preferences in contraception differ widely, and must, of course, be taken into account if adequate levels of acceptability and continuity are to be achieved. While it is true that there may never be an "ideal" contraceptive for all circumstances, it is clear that there should be a broader spectrum of methods which are safer, less discomforting, and more convenient; and which require less complex and costly distribution systems.

Such methods are well within the reach of biomedical science and adaptive technology, but will require sustained investigation and effort. Traditionally, reproductive research has been grossly underfinanced. Worldwide expenditures in 1975 were less than $130 million. Simply to maintain this wholly inadequate level of funding in the face of current inflation would mean approximately $200 million in 1980. But this is far below what is required. Two to three times that amount is needed, not merely because of the importance of the population issue itself, but because of the intrinsic time lags involved.

There a number of promising avenues for improved fertility regulation that have emerged from the basic research of the past fifteen years.[12] But even after a potential method has been developed, at least three to five years are required for testing before the method can be practically applied. And a wholly new discovery requires a full decade to reach the stage of a usable product.

What we must understand is that a variety of safe, effective, and acceptable methods of fertility regulation is not just needed now, and ten years from now, but in the years 2000, 2010, 2020 and so on. If new methods are to be available then, the research effort must be expanded now. And yet the field has been so starved for funds in recent years that more than half the approved grant applications for reproductive biological research have simply failed to be financed. Both the pharmaceutical industry and philanthropic foundations have been active in supporting such research, but they cannot be expected to carry the major funding expansion that is now urgently required. Governments must be prepared to direct substantially more effort in that direction.

The fruits of such research will result not only in better methods of contraception, but in the reduction of many other adverse medical and social effects of unwanted or abnormal pregnancy: prematurity, infant mortality, congenital defects, mental retardation, maternal morbidity and mortality—as well as illegitimacy, early marriage, family disruption, educational disadvantage, and the exacerbation of poverty.

The investment in reproductive research is immensely worthwhile. And there is simply no question that more or it is needed.[13] But, as I have indicated, this expanded research will require years of effort before it can be translated into radically different methods of contraception. Governments cannot afford simply to wait for that. Rather, they must in the meantime take action to improve present family planning programs and make broader use of current contraceptive technology. Such programs are necessary in all countries with rapidly expanding populations, regardless of the particular stage of economic and social development.

Family Planning in Relation to the Stages of Development
In some countries, widespread use of contraception precedes a change in desired family size, and may help it occur. In others, contraception becomes popular only after other factors have reduced family norms. But in either pattern, family planning is important, and indeed ultimately essential to meet the demand of parents for reduced family size.

In the lower-income developing countries, where absolute poverty is endemic, family planning programs should be shaped to service those parents who already desire to reduce their fertility; to urge others to consider that option; to increase local awareness of the damaging consequences of rampant population growth; and to recognize that by improving the health of the local community—and particularly of mothers and children—the program is in fact laying the foundation for a change in fertility norms.

Such an approach ensures that as the demand for family planning service increases, the supply is there to meet it. In the absence of more fundamental social and economic improvements, one cannot, of course, expect such a program to "solve" the population problem. But it would be equally naive to assume that it can have no effect on fertility whatever.

Indonesia, for example, is a particularly interesting case of a country with strong political commitment to fertility decline, and a vigorous family planning program, that appears to be off to a good start in spite of immense development problems.

In any event, the view that development in and by itself can take care of the fertility problem in the developing world is an unfortunate oversimplification as applied to most of the countries, and a dangerous error as applied to others. Even for the better-off developing countries, such a "development-only" strategy would we wasteful. The fall in fertility, without a strong family planning program, is likely to come later in the development process than it need to: per capita income would grow more slowly, and the ultimate size of the population would be larger.

But for the lower-income countries, a "development-only" strategy would be disastrous. In these countries it would take a much longer time to reach the socio-economic levels that normally correspond with significantly lower birth rates. Indeed in some of them, it is the very magnitude of the population pressures themselves that is retarding that progress. Were the fertility problem not dealt with directly, the progress would simply be too slow.

At the rate at which literacy has been increased and infant mortality and fertility reduced during the last decade, it would take India, for example, until the year 2010 to reach the literacy levels that normally correspond with crude birth rates of 30; and it would take until the year 2059 to reach the infant mortality levels that correspond with the CBR of 30.

If Nepal were to do nothing about its fertility directly, it would take it 170 years to reach the literacy level associated with a CBR of 30. India and Nepal—and many other countries—simply do not have that kind of time to experiment with a "development-only" strategy. And, happily, they have no intention of attempting it.

Whatever the rhetoric at Bucharest in 1974, no country has abandoned the anti-natalist policies it held then, and several have strengthened them.

Competent observers do argue about the relative importance of social development and family planning efforts in reducing fertility rates. Some say the former is too indirect. Others say the latter is too inefficient. But the truth is that the latest reviews of the experience of individual countries—reviews completed within the past twelve months—clearly support the conclusion that significant reduction of birth rates depends on both social development and family planning. The reviews suggest that family planning programs have a clear, substantial, and independent effect on country performance. Virtually all of the countries with reductions of 20%

or more in their crude birth rates during the decade 1965–1974 had strong family planning programs. But the research also confirms what common sense itself would suggest: that the effect of family planning programs is greatest when they are joined to efforts designed to promote related social goals.

Raising Population Consciousness

The real problem—for all of us—is to try to grasp the complexity of the population issue. Population problems are not simple; they are not straightforward; and they are certainly not very clear. They are like man himself: complicated. If we are to get down to solutions that really work, we have to try to see the problem in all its ramifications, and in all of its tangled interrelationships.

I recently asked a panel of distinguished experts to review our activities in the population field within the World Bank. They took a hard look at everything we have been doing since 1969, and they rightly reproached us for a tendency to treat population too much in isolation from our other activities. They pointed out that we have been prepared to lend for population projects, and were ready to bring specialized analysis to population issues when they were of obvious immediate importance. But too many of us in the Bank had proceeded as if population issues could be left to specilaists, rather than considered automatically in all aspects of our investment and development programs. In short, they asked us to think about the problem in a more comprehensive way—and deal with it accordingly. They were right. And that is exactly what we plan to do.

Let me, now, summarize and conclude the central points I have made this evening.

Summary and Conclusions

The argument I have made is this.

It now appears that a significant decline in fertility may have at last begun in the developing countries. The data are not yet fully conclusive, but the indications are that the crude birth rates have fallen over the past two decades by an average of about 6 points, or nearly 13 percent.

By major region, the decline has been 6.5 points in Asia; 5.4 points in Latin America; and 2.3 points in Africa.

Further, the decline appears to have been general and widespread. It has occurred in 77 of the 88 countries for which estimates are available.

If these indications are confirmed by the censuses scheduled for 1980, then what we are seeing here is something of historic importance. It would mean that the period of rapid acceleration in the rate of growth of the world's population has finally reached its peak and is now definitely moving downward towards stabilization.

But as welcome as this is, the fact remains that the current rate of decline in fertility in the developing countries is too slow to avoid their ultimately arriving at stationary populations far in excess of acceptable levels.

Unless governments, through appropriate policy action, can accelerate the reduction in fertility, the global population may not stabilize below 11 billion. That would be a world none of us would want to live in. But governments can take action, and can accelerate the process, given the resolve and determination to do so.

The critical point is this: for every decade of delay in achieving a net reproduction rate of 1.0—replacement-level fertility—the ultimate steady-state world population will be approximately 15 percent greater. Governments, then, must avoid the severe penalities of procrastination, and try to hasten the process forward. But how?

The causes and determinants of fertility reduction are extremely complex, but it appears likely that there are a number of key linkages between that reduction and certain specific elements of socioeconomic development.

The factors that appear to be the most important are: health, education, broadly distributed economic growth, urbanization, and the enhanced status of women. These factors are at work in the developing world today, but their progress is too slow to be fully effective.

Without additional intervention on the part of governments, the current population in the developing world is going to continue to grow at rates very substantially in excess of those that would permit far more economic and social progress.

There are two broad categories of interventions that governments must undertake: those designed to encourage couples to desire smaller families; and those designed to provide parents with the means to implement that desire.

The first set of interventions sets out to alter the social and economic environment that tends to promote fertility, and by altering it to create a demand among parents for a new and smaller family norm.

And the second set of interventions supplies the requisite means that will make that new norm attainable.

To create the demand for a change in family norm, governments should try to:

reduce current infant and child mortality rates sharply;

expand basic education and substantially increase the proportion of girls in school;

increase the productivity of smallholders in the rural areas, and expand earning opportunities in the cities for low-income groups;

put greater stress on more equitable distribution of income and services in the drive for greater economic growth;

and above all else, raise the status of women socially, economically, and politically.

To satisfy the demand for a change in family norms, governments and the international community should:

provide a broad choice of the present contraceptive techniques and services to parents;

improve the delivery systems by which parents can get the services they wish;

and expand present levels of research seeking better techniques and services.

Both categories of interventions are necessary.

Recent studies confirm that the effect of family planning programs is greatest when they are joined to efforts designed to promote related social goals.

We know that eventually the world's population will have to stop growing. That is certain. What is uncertain is how. And when. At what level. And with what result.

We who are alive today can determine the answers to those questions. By our action—or inaction—we will shape the world for all generations to come.

We can avoid a world of 11 billion, and all the misery that such an impoverished and crowded planet would imply. But we cannot avoid it by continuing into the next quarter century the ineffective approach to the problem of population that has characterized the past twenty-five years.

Man is still young in cosmic terms. He has been on earth for a million years or so. And our modern ancester, *Homo sapiens,* for a hundred thousand years. But the universe of which he is a part is some twenty billion years old. And if we represent the history of the universe by a line a mile long, then modern man has appeared on that line for only a fraction of an inch. In that time perspective, he is recent, and tentative, and perhaps even experimental. He makes mistakes. And yet, if he is truly *sapiens*—thinking and wise—then surely there is promise for him. Problems, yes. But very great promise—if we will but act.

Notes

1. There is, of course, a great range of differences between developing countries. Some have average life expectancies as low as 38; crude birth rates as high as 50 per 1,000; and annual growth rates as much as 3.5 percent, which double the population every 20 years. Women throughout these countries have an average number of children ranging between four and eight.

2. Total fertility levels in Mexico now exceed 6.0 children per female, compared to the replacement level of 2.3. Several decades of emphasis on population planning are likely to be required before replacement levels of fertility are reached.

3. I should stress that in choosing to speak on population, I do not mean to imply that it is the sole or predominant cause of social injustice and poverty. On several previous occasions, most recently in Manila, I have discussed the policy measures that governments of developing countries need to take to tackle poverty in both rural and urban areas. I have also reviewed the role that the developed nations must play through additional stimulus to international trade and higher levels of foreign assistance. To my mind, as later sections of this paper will demonstrate, policies to solve the poverty problem and to reduce the rate of population growth are complementary to each other: an effective attack on poverty is essential if population problems are going to be fully solved; and effective population policies are essential elements in the attack on poverty.

4. A typical example is the case of Algeria, as contrasted with Sweden. In Algeria, with its high birth rate, every 100 persons of working age in 1970 had to support 98 children under the age of 15. In Sweden, with its low birth rate, every 100 persons of working age had to support only 32 children under 15.

5. Recent research indicates there were some exceptions to the typical pattern of demographic transition. In some cases, the decline in fertility preceded the fall in mortality.

6. As Table 2 indicates, in many developing countries the effect of a decade of delay in achieving a NRR of 1.0 would not be a 15 percent increase in the steady-state population, but a 25 or 30 percent increase.

7. Mexico, for example, has moved since 1971 from a pro-natalist attitude on population to a vigorous family planning program with explicit demographic objectives.

8. Address to the Board of Governors of The World Bank, Nairobi, 1973.

9. Address to the Board of Governors of The World Bank, Washington, D.C., 1975.

10. One scheme proposed for Malaysia would make public assistance for the elderly available only for those parents with less than three children. Taiwan is experimenting with a bond system that will provide support for higher education of students in families with no more than three children. Singapore—a high-density island community—has designed a whole series of measures. In 1970, Prime Minister Lee Kuan Yew pointed out: "Beyond three children, the costs of subsidized housing, socialized medicine, and free education should be transferred to the parent."

11. From a child's point of view there can be few benefits in having many siblings. The close spacing of children and large numbers of children are likely to increase

infant and maternal mortality, and to worsen nutritional deficiencies and related health problems. This may in turn reduce a child's opportunity to benefit from whatever educational opportunities he has received. And in matters of inheritance, which in rural areas of some of the land-scarce countries is likely to be of critical importance even among very poor families, children from large families are at an obvious disadvantage.

12. Among these are better contraceptive methods for use by males. These could substantially improve the ability to regulate childbearing by giving husbands greater responsibility for contraception. Further, it would make it possible for couples to use alternate methods, and thus further reduce the risk of cumulative undesirable medical side effects.

13. The same need exists for additional social science research in the population field. There is a clear requirement to define more precisely those particular elements of social and economic development that most directly affect fertility.

Glossary

Crude Birth Rate (CBR): The number of live births, per year, per 1,000 of population.

Crude Death Rate (CDR): The number of deaths, per year, per 1,000 of population.

Rate of Natural Increase (NI): The difference between the crude birth rate and the crude death rate, usually expressed as a percentage.

Rate of Population Growth: The rate of natural increase, adjusted for migration, and expressed as a percentage of the total population in a given year.

Infant Mortality Rate: The number of deaths, per year, of infants aged 0–12 months, per 1,000 live births.

Life Expectancy at Birth: The average number of years newborn children would live if subject to mortality risks prevalent for the cross section of the population at the time of their birth.

General Fertility Rate: The number of live births per year, per 1,000 women, aged 15–49 years.

Total Fertility Rate (TRF): The number of children an average woman would have if during her lifetime her childbearing behavior were the same as that of the cross section of women at the time of observation. The TFR often serves as an estimate of the average number of children per family.

Gross Reproduction Rate (GRR): The number of daughters a woman would have under prevailing fertility patterns.

Net Reproduction Rate (NRR): The number of daughters a woman would have, under prevailing fertility and mortality patterns, who would survive to the mean age of childbearing.

Replacement-Level Fertility: A level of fertility equivalent to a Net Reproduction Rate of 1.0—the level at which childbearing women, on the average, have enough daughters to replace themselves in the population.

Stationary Population: A population that for a long time has had a constant replacement-level fertility and therefore also has a growth rate equal to zero and a constant age composition.

10

Arms, Energy, and the Atom: The Lethal Dilemma

Frank Church

I'm rather surprised at the lecture I've prepared because I wouldn't have thought that I would ever have come down on this side of the issue which I propose to discuss. Most of the time I have spent in the Senate I've been intensely interested in arms control and the effort to contain the atom. I am still extremely interested in that subject, and I agree with President Carter when he says that the problem of preventing the proliferation of nuclear weapons may be one of the most urgent of our time. Nevertheless, I must disagree with some of the conclusions that have been reached by the new administration in its efforts to grapple with this challenge.

In the background paper for these lectures there appears the following observation: "A central and new factor in the present world situation is that the exploitation of science and technology has so accelerated the rate of change of man's condition that our traditional means for dealing with political, economic, social, and military change are no longer adequate to the task."

This statement well describes the nuclear weapons proliferation dilemma. For here we have a classic case study of human technology outpacing our political capacity to tame the very atom which may either bestow energy salvation or lead us to destruction. It is this issue I wish to discuss.

I do so with trepidation. For me to discuss the complexities of nuclear technology at MIT is rather like going to the Mayo Clinic to lecture on open-heart surgery. Still, public policy, even in the most technical of fields, must ultimately be decided by elected officials. Every member of Congress must, therefore, do the best he can to grope with such subjects and communicate his conclusions to the public at large.

The administration's nuclear energy strategy has four major elements: (1) defer indefinitely nuclear fuel reprocessing; (2) restructure our nuclear

breeder program by deactivating the ongoing effort to bring about its com-
mercialization; (3) fund research and development in alternative fuel
cycles which, quoting the administration, "do not involve direct access to
materials usable in nuclear weapons"; and (4) increase substantially the
number of conventional nuclear power plants (the light water reactors),
together with our uranium enrichment capacity to fuel them both at home
and abroad. In effect, by deferring nuclear fuel reprocessing and the introduction of the breeder, the administration is attempting to avoid entering
the plutonium stage of nuclear energy development. Plutonium, it is felt,
increases the danger of nuclear weapons proliferation to an unacceptable
level of risk. By our unilateral renunciation of plutonium-based breeder
reactors and our offer to other nations of a guaranteed supply of enriched
uranium to fuel their conventional reactors, the administration hopes to
set an example which others will follow.

However well-intentioned, I am convinced that the administration's nuclear energy policy is a formula for nuclear isolationism. It will reduce, in
my judgment—not enhance—U.S. influence in shaping worldwide nuclear
policy. Thus, instead of advancing the control of nuclear weapons proliferation, our self-imposed restraint runs the grave risk of leaving an international vacuum, which is an invitation to nuclear anarchy.

I believe the administration proposal is flawed for at least two reasons.
First, it does not take sufficient account of the energy vulnerability of
countries lacking our resource base. The United States still produces nearly
60 percent of its oil needs, although imports have grown to alarming proportions. Moreover, we have massive coal reserves, oil shale potential and
large domestic uranium deposits. But other industrialized nations like
France, West Germany and Japan, and most developing countries, are not
so fortunate.

These energy-deficient countries have also been traumatized by the 600
percent rise in the price of oil mandated by the OPEC cartel since October
of 1973. During the past three years, the thirteen oil exporting nations of
OPEC have accumulated payments surpluses of $150 billion. The interest
alone on the consumer debt brought about by these huge surpluses
amounts to as much as the oil importers were paying for the oil itself
before 1970. And the debt keeps mounting. At the present time, the
OPEC governments are taking in about $45 billion more each year than
they can buy back in imports. Britain and Italy, borrowing to pay for their
oil, ran out of private credit last year. Portugal, Spain, Greece, and Turkey
are heading into trouble now, with Belgium, Denmark, and Finland not far
behind. France, practicing austerity, is still able to borrow privately. But

efforts to stimulate the French economy before next year's critical election will undoubtedly lift its import bill.

The breeder program is the only technology now on the horizon that holds out the promise of relieving Europe and Japan of an unremitting dependence upon foreign-held fuel supplies. The singular advantage of the breeder is that future models, on the basis of known technology, should produce more fuel than they consume. A breeder program makes possible the use of the otherwise worthless uranium 238 (which comprises 99.3 percent of natural uranium), and this becomes a potential fuel resource of incalculable value. Indeed, the United States already has in storage tons of tailings containing purified uranium 238 which, if used in a breeder program, could produce an electrical equivalent five times larger than all the oil in the Middle East!

Neither the governments in Western Europe nor Japan are going to remain bound in an energy straitjacket if they have a chance to achieve, through a breeder program, eventual energy independence. John Anderson, the energy specialist for *The Washington Post,* after a trip to major European capitals, concluded:

The major European powers have already gone a very long way in their commitment to the development of the plutonium breeder reactor. France and Britain have both had experimental breeders running since the 60s. Germany has one in operation now, and there's another under construction in Italy. As for the much bigger commercial breeders, France has now decided to go ahead with the world's first—the 1200-megawatt Superphoenix. A 1300-megawatt breeder is under design in Britain.
But they won't be competitive, in economic terms, unless they are widely used. There is going to be a fierce pressure on European governments to export these machines, to help defray the enormous development costs. The German sale of the plutonium reprocessing plant to Brazil isn't the last of these cases. It's more likely to be only the first.

The second flaw in the administration's program, as I see it, is that it fails to offer a satisfactory substitute for the world's diminishing supply of oil. According to a CIA study made public recently, global oil supplies will begin to fall short of world demand by 1985, a few short years away! In the face of this dire forecast, the administration hopes to persuade other nations to stick with conventional reactors and agree to "one-use-only" of the enriched uranium with which they are run. Such a "throw-away" policy involves burying the used fuel rods with the unspent uranium and newly-created plutonium still inside, after they are removed from a nuclear power plant.

Inasmuch as the spent fuel rods can be reprocessed and recycled through the reactors again (adding 30 percent to the energy originally produced),

and since the plutonium manufactured by the fission process could fuel
the breeder (thus assuring the world an ample energy source for generations to come), the Administration's plan is viable only if the supply of
natural uranium were virtually unlimited.

This, of course, is anything but the case. The administration relies upon
a Ford Foundation study which assumes that there will be far more re-
coverable uranium found in this country than intensive exploration has
indicated. The Ford study estimates a 3.7 million ton reserve figure. But a
series of studies by federal agencies, including one conducted by the National Academy of Sciences, have concluded that the known and probable
reserves of uranium in this country total about 1.8 million tons. Such a
quantity would provide only one-half of the nuclear energy production
required by the United States alone between now and the end of the century. Even if the optimistic Ford Foundation prediction proved true, it is
still apparent that the United States would be unable to produce, from its
own natural uranium deposits, a sufficient supply of enriched uranium to
meet our own needs and those of our foreign customers, besides. We ask,
in effect, that by abandoning the breeder, they exchange one depleting
source of fuel, oil, for another, natural uranium. How can we expect them
to do it?

Moreover, recent disclosures have shown that the foreign uranium production market may be susceptible to cartelization by a few producers.
Prices have jumped to OPEC-type levels, so much so that the Westing-
house Corporation is now enmeshed in litigation which endangers its sol-
vency as it was forced to renege on uranium supply contracts which had
assumed relatively stable prices. In short, it is unrealistic to believe that
other fuel-deficient governments are going to confine themselves to a
multi-billion dollar conventional reactor program, while relying upon a
future supply of natural uranium which is unsure in quantity and susceptible to drastic price manipulation.

So we should not be surprised that oil-deficient nations are even now
turning in the opposite direction, toward protectionist energy policies.

A Brazilian government white paper on nuclear energy summed up this
sentiment:

Recent historical developments have demonstrated the dangers of relying
heavily on external sources for the satisfaction of the basic input needs of
the economy . . . . To avoid what happened in the case of oil—it was imperative that the solution in the case of nuclear energy be one that enabled
the country to reach the indispensable autarky in the medium term.

In other words, it was not acceptable to replace one form of dependence
for another—the economic growth of the country, or its mere subsistence,

cannot be dependent upon third countries' decisions as to prices and supplies of essential fuels.

So, like it or not, in the post-OPEC world breeder reactor has become the symbol of the nationalist drive for energy independence. If there was any doubt on this score, surely it must have been dispelled by the recent West German government announcement approving a four-year, $2.7 billion program of energy research, focusing on nuclear-power and plutonium-based reactors.

As against the energy potential of the breeder program and the reprocessing stage which is necessary as preliminary to the breeder, the administration has cited the danger of nuclear weapons proliferation. It is important, therefore, to try to understand precisely what that danger is. Halting nuclear energy short of the plutonium stage will not eliminate the risk of proliferation. As the Ford Foundation study itself observed, the requirements for making nuclear weapons can be reduced to three: (1) uranium, (2) trained personnel, and (3) facilities to produce enriched uranium or plutonium from the natural uranium.

While uranium is unevenly distributed and most countries are dependent on imports, relatively little is needed to manufacture a bomb. Indeed, India obtained the requisite amounts from the imported fuel for its small research reactor. Most of the technology necessary for a weapons program is readily available to scientists and engineers. The Ford study acknowledged that a weapons program is "certainly within the capabilities of developed countries, and of many developing countries." And, although a very large investment has so far been required for uranium enrichment, new methods on a much smaller scale are in various stages of development. Today, it is easily within the means of any of a dozen advanced non-nuclear weapons states to build a centrifuge plant adequate for a modest weapons program.

As Representative McCormack noted in a recent article in *The Washington Post:*

The reason that weapons have not been made from commercial nuclear power plant fuel is that it is much cheaper and simpler to make nuclear weapons from natural uranium using facilities designed and built exclusively for that purpose. Trying to divert nuclear power plant fuel into weapons production is the most expensive, clumsy, dangerous and inefficient way for any nation to make a weapon.

For these reasons, I believe that our energy policy must feature the reprocessing of spent fuel in the near future, accompanied by the research and development necessary to enable us, by the early 1990s, to place on the market some form of breeder technology. At the same time, I believe that this country must take the lead in strengthening and extending existing institutions like the International Atomic Energy Agency. We must do what we fell short of doing in the 1950s and 1960s, namely, devise an international framework which will enable all non-weapons states to meet their genuine energy needs with nuclear power, while minimizing the risk of nuclear weapons proliferation.

The problem now, as I see it, is to devise an effective system of international controls. If we begin by laying down an American commandment: "Thou shalt not have access to nuclear reprocessing and possess breeder reactors," not only will we fail, but we will exacerbate nationalistic passions and lose the opportunity to build upon the embryonic international institutions which now exist.

Almost twenty-five years ago, the United States admitted that we could not prevent other countries from acquiring and developing nuclear technology. In his "Atoms-for-Peace" address to the United Nations on December 8, 1953, President Eisenhower outlined a new American policy based upon the recognition of this truth. He proposed the creation of a new organization under the UN to assist countries in developing nuclear energy for peaceful purposes. Recipients of this assistance were to agree to international inspection, in order to prevent the diversion of materials for weapons use. As the world leader in nuclear technology, the United States sought to influence the peaceful development of this vast new energy source while at the same time restricting its use in the building of weapons arsenals.

So we took the lead in the creation of the International Atomic Energy Agency (IAEA). Ever since, that agency, with our strong support, has furnished technical assistance and materials to participating countries and has developed and administered a system of safeguards. Meanwhile, the United States, carrying out its commitments under the IAEA Statute and the Treaty on the Non-Proliferation of Nuclear Weapons, has helped other countries acquire research and power reactors. We have been the world's major supplier of nuclear materials, equipment, technology and training. But the infant system of international inspection and control that we fathered has not kept pace with the growing need.

I would therefore suggest that we abandon any new and demonstrably futile attempt to contain the flow of nuclear technology and try instead to channel it in directions that will provide adequate supplies of energy while minimizing the potential for making nuclear weapons. We should aim toward eventual international ownership and control of the fuel cycle necessary to sustain commercial reactors in all non-weapons states. Regional uranium-enrichment and reprocessing plants should be established under the auspices of the IAEA. This agency should own all the nuclear fuel in its global system, be responsible for the fuel's security, and accountable for its use. Fuel elements could be leased to the participating nations on the condition that the spent rods would be returned, and that each reactor in which they are inserted would be subject to IAEA inspection.

No plutonium or other weapons material would ever be produced in a form which could be used for weapons fabrication; the fuel would be blended with other materials to make it unworkable for bomb construction. For example, the reprocessing would produce only blended uranium and plutonium, usable for fuel elements, but unworkable in a weapon.

Fuel fabricating facilities would be built immediately adjacent to the chemical separation plant, as would a facility for glassification of all end waste for deep burial. New fuel elements could be slightly irradiated as a last step before being shipped from the facility. Thus, they would require the same heavy shielding that is necessary to return irradiated fuel elements from a nuclear power plant.

Such a system of international supply and control would not only provide maximum protection against diverting fuel to weapons but would meet the legitimate demands of the non-weapons states for an assured supply of nuclear fuel at a fair price. Just as the American government now sells enriched uranium to commercial reactors in this country, the IAEA could make its fuel available to participating states at cost.

The system I have described would also furnish the best insurance against terrorists. By dealing only in irradiated fuel, it would be necessary to steal at least one, and perhaps several, 50-ton shipping casks in order to obtain enough material to make a single weapon. Furthermore, it would be necessary to extract the weapons material from the hot fuel rods, a feat requiring elaborate facilities. This should reduce the potential for illicit diversion for weapons materials virtually to zero.

Now, I do not underestimate the formidable task of establishing such a global system. But while we work in that direction, our national policies should constitute the example of how such a system might work. In this regard, I agree with Congressman Mike McCormack, the chairman of the House Science and Technology Subcommittee, who recently observed:

Of course no system is perfect or foolproof. It should be obvious, however, that this nation and the world can have the energy required for economic stability and a high degree of nuclear security as well.

If some nation decides that, in spite of all the attendant problems, it is determined to obtain nuclear weapons, then it will obviously be much easier to make the weapons outside the fuel cycle, as was done by India.

This could be done secretly today, regardless of any restraints the United States places on its own energy programs. It is more likely to happen if the United States does not provide leadership for a workable program to assure adequate controls and supplies of energy.

Above all else, this nation must lead, and from a credible position. The other nations of the world do not believe that we can provide them with nuclear fuel unless we have a breeder program and unless we recycle and reprocess our fuel.

These are the reasons that I must conclude that the administration's program will not work.

Index